# Odd Birds

# IAN HARDING

# Odd Birds

ST. MARTIN'S PRESS ❧ NEW YORK

ODD BIRDS. Copyright © 2017 by Ian Harding. All rights reserved.
Printed in the United States of America. For information, address
St. Martin's Press, 175 Fifth Avenue, New York, N.Y. 10010.

www.stmartins.com

Designed by Anna Gorovoy

Title-page illustrations by Jim Tierney

Library of Congress Cataloging-in-Publication Data

Names: Harding, Ian, 1986– author.
Title: Odd birds / Ian Harding.
Description: First edition. | New York : St. Martin's Press, 2017.
Identifiers: LCCN 2017001939 | ISBN 9781250117076 (hardcover) |
    ISBN 9781250156488 (signed edition) | ISBN 9781250117083 (ebook)
Subjects: LCSH: Harding, Ian, 1986– | Actors—United States—
    Biography. | Birds watching—Anecdotes. | BISAC: BIOGRAPHY &
    AUTOBIOGRAPHY / Entertainment & Performing Arts. | NATURE /
    Animals / Birds. | BIOGRAPHY & AUTOBIOGRAPHY / Rich &
    Famous.
Classification: LCC PN2287.H225 A3 2017 | DDC 791.4502/8092 [B]—dc23
LC record available at https://lccn.loc.gov/2017001939

Our books may be purchased in bulk for promotional, educational,
or business use. Please contact your local bookseller or the Macmillan
Corporate and Premium Sales Department at 1-800-221-7945, extension 5442,
or by e-mail at MacmillanSpecialMarkets@macmillan.com.

First Edition: May 2017

10  9  8  7  6  5  4  3  2  1

For Bubs.
Always.

# Contents

Large and isolated in the gleaming whiteness of the page, the hawk stares back at you, bold, statuesque, brightly coloured. But when you have shut the book, you will never see that bird again. Compared with the close and static image, the reality will seem dull and disappointing. The living bird will never be so large, so shiny-bright. It will be deep in landscape, and always sinking farther back, always at the point of being lost. Pictures are waxworks beside the passionate mobility of the living bird.

—J. A. Baker, *The Peregrine*

# Odd Birds

# Introduction

## BRIDGE

## TO NOWHERE

The day had been sweltering. I'd spent the last few hours trying to avoid the heat, but as I stood in the river, the icy cold water rushing around my ankles, I began to shiver.

I looked up and down the river. I couldn't find the bird.

A blur tracked across my peripheral vision. I turned to see where it went.

Large boulders interrupted the river in places, and looking out over the water, I couldn't see where the bird had landed. It had been only a shadow of a motion—a flash of gray.

Where the hell had it gone?

Maybe it had landed just out of sight, I figured, so I began to slog through the river, periodically glancing upstream to see if it had landed on any of the boulders sticking out of the water. Bird-less, every last one of them.

Maybe the bird had flown farther upstream than I had realized, and here I was, standing in a river, my teeth chattering, just a bit overeager to find it.

I looked out at the river again and tried to take it all in. White riffles coursed around the large boulders. The water was fast-moving and clear where it had room to flow. A trout rose to the surface of a pool below one of the rocks.

There it was again. The flash of gray.

As I turned to look, the movement congealed into the form of a small bird, its tail bobbing rhythmically as it perched out on a boulder in the middle of the water. It turned back and forth, looking upstream and down, as if trying to make up its mind where to go.

The bird hop-flew to the next rock downstream, toward me, and continued to bob its tail. It blinked—I saw it blink—its white eyelids popping against its slate-gray body.

An American dipper. This was a good bird.


I had gotten a late start that morning. It was a Saturday in August, and I was driving out of Los Angeles—the city I call home. I was going up to the mountains to go hiking and birding by myself, then I had plans to meet up with friends to camp for the night.

I turned the AC up to full blast as I drove: it was a stupefyingly hot day in the Southland.

I've been in LA for just under a decade now, and I love it here. An ocean to the west, mountains to the north. The city stretches east and south, and the mass of humanity here seems more or less continuous all the way down to San Diego. There's a lot to do close by—you can surf in the morning in Santa

Monica and then drive two hours to spend the afternoon skiing at Big Bear.

Los Angeles County is huge—substantially larger than the city itself. It stretches far north over the Angeles National Forest and the San Gabriel Mountains, encompassing Antelope Valley—which blooms orange with California poppies in the spring—the eastern corner of the Los Padres National Forest, and the western corner of the Mojave Desert. Despite the urban sprawl across large parts of the county, which is home to more than ten million people, even larger swathes are covered in oak woodland, pine and fir forest, and desert—and there's seventy miles of coastline.

Because of the diversity of habitat, you can see more species of birds in Los Angeles County than almost anywhere else in the United States.

A little more than an hour on the road, I exited the 210 at Azusa. I was on my way to the Angeles National Forest, which includes the mountain range to the northeast of the city. A few turns put me on the 39, heading north into the park.

As the highway switchbacked up off the valley floor, I started to think about my plan for the weekend. Today I was looking forward to getting outdoors, roughing it for a night. In the morning I would wake up early to drive back to Los Angeles. A stylist was coming over to my house in the midafternoon to make me look presentable, because tomorrow night I was attending the Teen Choice Awards.

For the past seven years I've played a high school English teacher named Ezra Fitz on a TV show called *Pretty Little Liars*. It was a gig I was fortunate enough to land right out of college. Right now, I'm finishing up filming on the last season of *PLL*—its seventh.

As I drove, I thought back to an idea I'd had for a while—three seasons back, my character on the show wrote a book, and I've been thinking about writing one myself ever since. What you're reading now is the result of that crazy idea.

This book isn't a chronological memoir. I'm too young to write something like that anyway. Instead, it's a collection of stories and thoughts I've had about my life in Hollywood and my life outdoors—and a few things I've only recently been able to put words to.

I want to look back on my experiences so far and talk about a few of them: about my childhood, about my life as an actor, and about some of the things I find meaningful. And, yes, birds. A lot about birds. Because they mean a lot to me, and they keep cropping up in my life.

As I continued up into the park, I had to concentrate fully on the winding road. All around loomed mountains covered in chaparral, a tangle of thorns and brush, brown and faded gray-green, vegetation the color of desert camouflage.

A cyclist was pushing himself up and up and up the steep road, and I followed behind him for a ways, watching his legs turn pedals turn gears turn wheels, waiting for a sight line long enough to safely pass.

And then, farther along, the road twisted back on itself, and I got a view back down the valley—where I had been fifteen minutes earlier—and I saw the haze of the heat rising off the endless city, and the thin layer of smog hugging the land below the clear air of the mountains.

I wasn't close to my destination yet, but somehow it felt like I had arrived.

———

I pulled off the road at a ranger station to see if I could get a recommendation for a hike. The ranger at the station was more goat than man. He had a scraggly white patch of fur under his chin and was wearing a pair of indoor-outdoor glasses—the kind that are always tinted purplish gray, even indoors.

"Hi there," I said, approaching the counter. "I'm looking for a short day hike. Something a few miles long."

"You got enough water?" the ranger asked, not looking up from the newspaper he was reading. "Need a couple of liters today. The sun's brutal."

I know park rangers have to deal with people with death wishes on a near-daily basis, but I know the rules: Take nothing but selfies, leave nothing but footprints. And always carry plenty of water.

"Yup, I've got a couple of bottles," I said. The ranger glanced up from his paper, looked me over, and rolled his eyes.

He pulled out a map of the park, pointing out where we were. Farther up the road, past the spot where my friends and I were planning to camp that night, he pointed to a parking lot on the map.

"This is Coyote Flat. Park here—if the lot is full, park along the road. There's a five-miler here that'll take you to the Bridge to Nowhere."

Perfect. While the name "Bridge to Nowhere" wasn't particularly auspicious, a five-mile hike was just what the doctor ordered.*

———

* I later realized that, to this particular park ranger, "five-miler" meant "five miles each way," which was not quite what the doctor ordered. But at the time I was unaware of this fact.

I glanced at my phone before getting back into the car. I knew I was about to lose the little bit of reception I still had, but I wasn't concerned. John and Walter, the two friends I was meeting up with later that night, knew where we were supposed to meet. I was actually looking forward to being unreachable for a few hours.

Twenty minutes later, I parked in a large lot—it was mostly empty—and started off down a dirt path at the far end. The sun was at its apex, and the temperature must have been in the high nineties.

It was a dry, mind-scrambling heat, like the physical embodiment of white noise—and there was no breeze or even rustle of wind. I slathered sunblock all over my face, and would've dunked my head into a vat of it if they sold containers large enough.

I started up the trail, which follows the east fork of the San Gabriel River.

Walking along, the crunch of gravel underfoot seemed especially loud. You pay closer attention to your surroundings when you hike alone, and even the sound of a twig snapping can make you jump—at least until you get used to being back in the food chain.

The trail dropped steadily from the parking lot for half a mile to a campground set among a small stand of pine trees. There were a few tents scattered about. Some were just tarps draped over cords, others seemed built for more permanent residence, and had strings of laundry hanging out to dry.

Passing through that brief bit of shade under the trees was a welcome reprieve. But then the trail left the trees and the road behind to parallel the course of the river, crossing over it from time to time.

A few hundred yards past the campsite, I realized I hadn't heard any birds. No canyon wrens, no scrub jays—nothing. Too hot for them to be singing, apparently. I was starting to feel a little light-headed myself, and I wondered if it was such a good idea to be outside for so long. I had two liters of water on me, which I figured was more than enough. I took a swig from one of my wide-mouthed Nalgenes.

I could feel my face beginning to burn. I opened up my pack and pulled out a balaclava, which I originally bought for skiing because it covers my entire face—except a thin slit for my eyes. It's also great for sun protection while out hiking, as long as you don't mind looking like a yuppie jihadist. The occasional odd looks are worth the protection from skin cancer.

I took the Nalgene I was drinking from and poured it over my head to cool off, and then reached for the other I'd brought along. To my utter horror, it was empty. I'd forgotten to fill it up. At the next water crossing, I jumped into the river in my clothes to cool off, which was nice, for a moment. Above the crossing, a trio of unkempt redneck "entrepreneurs" in their early thirties was shoveling soil into a sluice box—it looked to be a small-time gold-panning operation.

The water around me was filthy—full of the runoff from their work. I hadn't been planning on it, but now I definitely wasn't going to drink from the stream.

"Finding anything?" I called over to them, trying to be friendly.

They stared at me for a moment. One coughed. They went back to their work.

Sometimes it's hard to make good conversation in the woods. People mostly come here to be left alone.

I realized then that I still had the balaclava on, and must've been a weird sight, sitting there in the river, lightly panting. The men continued to ignore me, and I took my cue to keep walking, a little soggier now, my shoes squishing with each step and the bottoms slowly caking with sandy soil.

I slogged onward, my eyes focused on the ground. I tried not to think about how thirsty I was. The river floodplain widened out, and yucca plants festooned the flats like Koosh balls. I found myself slowly following a path up the eastern side of the valley.

Where the hell was this bridge? Around every turn in the trail, more trail . . . and I was completely out of water.

The sun continued to torment. I kept putting one foot in front of the other, willing them to move more out of spite than muscle memory.

I passed a pair of hikers on their way back down: a mother and her teenage daughter.

"You're almost there!" the mom said encouragingly.

I guess my balaclava didn't frighten everyone after all. I nodded a quick thanks and picked up the pace. I was getting somewhere after all.

I'd gone another fifteen steps or so when I heard a voice call out from behind me—"Ian?"

I stopped and turned around. The teenage girl and her mom were standing in the middle of the path looking back at me. The girl's hands were shaking.

"Ian?" the girl said again. I stared at her, dumbfounded. How on earth could she have recognized me? My face was almost completely covered—all she could see were my eyes.

I couldn't recognize my own mother by only her eyes.

"Uh . . . yes?" I managed to stammer.

Her face lit up. "I knew it!" she cried. Before I knew what was happening, she was hugging me. My clothes were damp from sweat and river water.

"Nice to see you, too," I said.

"This is so exciting!" she chirped. "I'm a huge fan of your show."

I looked down and saw that the girl was carrying a canteen.

"Can I have some of your water?" I blurted out.

They both seemed taken aback.

"Um . . . okay," the girl said, reaching for her canteen and handing it to me. I thanked her and took a few desperate gulps.

"Would it be possible to take a picture with you?" she asked.

"Sure, of course," I said, handing her back her canteen.

The mom took out her iPhone. I put my arm around the girl's shoulder and smiled. The mom held the screen up to her face, framing the picture, then hesitated and put it down. "Everything okay?" I asked.

"Would you mind taking off your face mask?"

I had forgotten all about it again.

After we took the photo, I thanked the mother and daughter for the water and hiked on, hoping that I'd soon reach my destination. I was beginning to worry that the Bridge to Nowhere might not actually exist.

But then, not fifteen minutes later, around a corner, there it was.

Turns out it wasn't some big metaphor, after all. It was real.

The bridge was beautiful—a Depression-era concrete arch that spanned a deep gorge—and far below, a clear mountain stream carried snowmelt down to the valley below.

When the bridge was originally constructed, in 1936, it was intended to connect the north side of Angeles National Forest with the south. Partway through construction, the road leading up to the bridge was washed out by a massive flood. Rebuilding the road was subsequently deemed not worth it, leaving the bridge orphaned in the middle of the wilderness.

There was a hand-pump spigot on the bridge, and I doused my head under it. After thoroughly soaking my hair, I filled my water bottles and collapsed in a sweaty heap under a canvas sunshade that was stretched out over the bridge.

My head was still burning up, that feverish buzzing of dehydration. I closed my eyes for a second and must have dozed off.

When I snapped back to reality, there were three or four other hikers loafing around nearby. Two of them sat, backs against the concrete wall of the bridge, eating cans of Vienna sausage. In a cooler at their feet, I noticed a stack of empty sausage tins.

Off in the distance, a pair of ravens cruised by, their wedge-shaped tails pronounced in stark outline against the summer sun.

I stood up and stretched my legs. I considered walking back down, but I found myself looking to the far side of the bridge. I didn't feel like going back down just yet, so I got up and wandered across.

On the other side of the Bridge to Nowhere, there was a trail, a path to the river below. Picking my steps carefully, I made my way down to the water.

As I stood looking up and down the river, taking it all in, the colors and textures, I thought back to the girl and her mother I'd met on the trail. I replayed the interaction in my head, still amazed that she'd been able to recognize me with that balaclava on.

Had I been rude? I hoped not. I'd definitely come across as disoriented. A little weird, probably. At worst, they walked away thinking I was on drugs—and I could live with that.

A blur tracked across my peripheral vision—I turned to see what it was. It was a motion, a flash of gray. I couldn't find it.

You know what happens next.

I stumbled downstream, planting a foot squarely into the river in my frantic search to find the bird. And there it was again: the American dipper.

There's no wrong way to look at birds.

You can go to the coast and set up a scope and pan across the ocean's edge, looking for shorebirds. You can walk through the woods and listen—identifying them by their songs. You can watch them on feeders in your backyard from your living room, taking in the beauty of their myriad forms.

You can take a reference book out to the woods and compare the pictures to the birds that you see in the wild. You can learn about their field marks—the shape of their tails or the way they bob up and down.

Often though, the birds don't stay put long enough for you to observe them as much as you'd want. Instead, what you see is a motion. Birds aren't static objects, and birding makes you good at identifying blurs.

Sometimes I let my eyes not focus on anything in particular—let them almost glaze over, fall out of focus, and take it all in—and then the motion will register, like a water bug skating across a glassy surface. Out in the forest, or even just walking around my neighborhood, I'll see the motion before I actually see the bird.

But, when my eyes do pick up on that motion, I'm able to trace the bird as it moves through the trees or arcs across the sky.

You learn very quickly to key in on forms. Size alone can be deceiving—depth perception doesn't work as well when a bird is set against an endless expanse of blue sky. You look for the little details, like the shape of the crest—and whether it is rounded or squared off. Or even how it flies. Three undulating wing-flaps, then a wide, gliding dip? Good chance that's a woodpecker.

As a birder, you develop a rough sense of the birds you could see in any given area, so you can know almost immediately when something's unusual because it doesn't fit the forms you're expecting to find.

I sat down on a rock, my shoes dripping, and watched the dipper hop around the stream, disappearing beneath the water's surface from time to time to walk across the bottom of the riverbed, searching for food.

Then the air changed and a cool gust of wind came down the river, ruffling the bird's feathers.

I looked up. The sun had started to set behind the mountains to the west. Shade stretched across the gorge, and there was a sudden chill in the air. I looked at my watch and realized it was getting late. It would be dark soon. Before long, my friends would arrive at the campsite down below.

We would spend the night talking around the campfire, looking at the stars and wondering what the different constellations meant. Later, we would climb into our tents and fall fast asleep, enveloped by the chirping and howls of the mountains around us.

In the morning I would drive back to Los Angeles for the awards ceremony. In the evening I would be on the red carpet, posing and laughing with my costars.

But now? Now I would hike down, into the darkening night, to be with my friends, and fall asleep beneath the stars.

# FAMILY

## CARDINALS

When I was a kid, my mom told me to keep an eye out for cardinals whenever I went out to play in the woods behind our house.

"They look out for us," she told me. "So we need to look out for them, too."

Cardinals hold a very special place in my family, and much of our family folklore centers around them. I'm reminded of this whenever I go back to Maryland to visit my mom—you can't find cardinals in Los Angeles, they don't make it this far west.

My mom keeps porcelain statuettes of them on shelves and tabletops around the house. She has cardinal coffee mugs, picture frames decorated with cardinals, even cardinal-themed oven mitts. At Christmas, cardinal ornaments overwhelm the tree.

They brighten up her house in much the same way the real birds can appear as a bloom of crimson on a snowy winter's day.

My mom inherited her name, Mary, from her mother, and her love of cardinals from her father, John Collins.

Grandpa John served in the army during World War II. He received a Purple Heart and Silver Star for storming a fortified hillside to hurl a grenade into a Nazi pillbox. After the war, he returned to Virginia, where he met his wife, Mary, and started a family.

John and Mary were Irish Catholic, and they brought their children up in the Church. The family always had a particular fondness for saints and guardian angels. They were always looking for symbols of their faith in their lives—signs of divine presence in the world around them.

Grandpa John was also an amateur naturalist and a history buff, and he loved the cardinal because it was the state bird of Virginia—never mind the fact that it's also the state bird of five other states. He would always point the birds out to his kids when they appeared in the yard. At some point, my mom and her siblings came to believe that cardinals were the guardian angels of the Collins family.

I never met my grandmother Mary. She died of pancreatic cancer when my mom was eleven years old.

According to my mom, the week after her mother's funeral, a female cardinal flew up and perched right outside the dining room while the family was eating breakfast. The bird seemed to be peering in through the window, watching over my mom and her siblings as they ate. My grandfather noticed, and as he pointed the bird out to his kids, it began to sing— its syrupy call inserting itself into the conversation like my grandmother used to do.

Eventually, my grandfather remarried. His new wife, Alice, was squat in appearance and cranky in demeanor. She took on the job of parenting my mother and her siblings as best she could.

So now there was Grandpa John and Grandma Alice in the house—and a cardinal that acted suspiciously like Grandma Mary living in the backyard.

Fast-forward a few decades. I was in elementary school. Grandpa John got sick. Mom, being a nurse, could tell that he wasn't going to get better.

A few days after Grandpa John died, a pair of cardinals showed up at the feeder we had hanging in our backyard.

We'd often hear them calling before they appeared. They'd come in from the forest to the bushes at the edge of the lawn and survey the house. Then, in stuttered flight, they'd swoop across the yard. The cardinals would take turns at the feeder, one perching to eat while the other hopped around the ground below.

My mom liked to believe—we all liked to believe—that it was Grandpa John and Grandma Mary, reunited as cardinals in the afterlife.

Grandma Alice never remarried, and became less cranky with age. I loved spending time with her, and we used to sit and talk for hours. Actually, let me rephrase that: I would talk for hours, and she would smile and nod. She said she didn't believe in hearing aids, and I don't think she could hear a word I said.

Halfway through my freshman year of college, Grandma Alice passed away.

Back home in Virginia, the same pair of cardinals that had appeared when Grandpa John died was still coming around—they were still regulars at the feeder. Or at least we thought they were the same birds. The male had an especially dark mask, and the female's crest was a bright red—brighter than I'd seen on other birds.

The morning after Alice's funeral—as we were standing in the kitchen trying to figure out what to do with all the leftover food from the memorial reception—a new cardinal appeared. It was another female, and it sat at the feeder alongside the original pair.

This bird was different from the others. She was squat and a little drab, and even appeared cranky, becoming aggressive with birds twice her size when they came too close to her food.

So, naturally, we concluded, these cardinals were Grandpa John, Grandma Mary, and Grandma Alice.

It was fun to imagine that our loved ones had embodied birds so they could come back and look after us. But we never took the cardinal symbolism *that* seriously. I'm not a superstitious person, and for my sister and me, the cardinals were just a coincidence: coincidences happen.

If you pressed me, though, I do have a cardinal story of my own.

It was the winter before I graduated from college. I was driving back to Pittsburgh from Virginia, where I'd spent the holidays with my family. The whole world was gray outside, and it was beginning to snow.

Despite the weather, I was booking it back to the 'Burgh. I was making my way up a long hill when a glint of red came out of the trees along the highway. I could just make out the cardinal through the snow, flapping its way across the road in front of my car.

I slowed and changed lanes to avoid hitting the bird, and as I did, the back tire of an eighteen-wheeler directly in front of me blew out. The truck swerved violently into the other lane, right where I'd been seconds before. If I hadn't hit the brakes to avoid that cardinal, the truck would've crushed me.

A few years later I mentioned what had happened to my mom. She just smiled and nodded. "These things happen," she said.

When I was in elementary school, my mom got sick. Really sick. Nobody could figure out what was wrong. She went to a bunch of different specialists, but they all struggled to diagnose her illness. In the meantime, she was told to rest and drink plenty of fluids.

She spent weeks in bed, exhausted. Moving hurt. Talking hurt. She would break out in rashes whenever she went out in the sun. And then the rash would be replaced by a fever and her joints would swell up. More doctors' appointments, spinal taps, and blood tests all came back inconclusive. At one point she was diagnosed with meningitis, only to have the diagnosis reversed a week later.

We didn't know it yet, but my mom had lupus.

Lupus is a difficult disease to diagnose—and is done so mostly by process of elimination. And, even after it is diagnosed, there still isn't a cure.

When my mom found out she had lupus, little was known about the disease. She was told that the remainder of her shortened life—perhaps only another ten years—would consist of rapid and violent swings of health, and constant joint and intestinal pain.

Instead of resigning herself to her diagnosis, she decided to fight back on all fronts. She proceeded to eat cleaner than a triathlete, tried every immunosuppressive drug on the market, and prayed harder than the pope.

Since her diagnosis more than twenty years ago, my mom's dietary and healthcare choices seem to have been working. To this day, she has remained in reasonably good health.

But lupus is still an insidious disease. At times it acts as though it has a mind of its own.

I went home for Christmas several years ago to spend the holidays with my mom and her sister, Julie. There was a bunch of family in town, and it was lovely to all be together. Christmas is my mom's favorite holiday, so we all went to bed early on Christmas Eve. Everyone wanted the next day to arrive as soon as possible.

Early the next morning, Aunt Jules shook me awake—it was still dark outside.

"There's something wrong with your mom," she said.

I ran to my mom's room and found her sitting up in bed, thumbing her rosary with one hand and taking her blood pressure with the other.

She looked up at me, her body shaking. "It feels like I'm having a heart attack." Her breathing was shallow, forced. "But it isn't a damn heart attack," she said.

My mom worked as a cardiac nurse practitioner for several years—she knew all the signs. And she was right: it wasn't a heart attack. She was having a lupus flare. A bad one.

The paramedics arrived quickly—wearing Santa hats—and they lifted her out of bed and carried her down the stairs.

We spent Christmas morning in the hospital with her, while the doctors ran a battery of tests to see what might have triggered the flare. By that afternoon, she said she was feeling well enough to go home, so they gave her some pain medication and released her.

My mom's recovery over the next few days was painful and slow. She seemed older, frailer than I'd seen her before. I asked if she wanted me to delay my flight back to Los Angeles, but she insisted that I shouldn't change anything on her behalf.

On the morning of my departure, I went for a run to clear my head. When I got back to the house, I heard laughter coming from upstairs. At first I thought it might be Aunt Jules, but my mom's guffaw is unmistakable.

I went upstairs and knocked on the bedroom door.

"Come in," she said. Her voice sounded warmer, stronger.

I stepped into the room to find her rolled onto her side in bed, looking out the window. She waved me over. I sat down on the edge of the bed and we both looked out.

There they were: the three cardinals, Grandpa John, Grandma Mary, and cranky Grandma Alice. They were all perched in the branches of a tree that brushed up against the side of the house.

Grandpa John's mouth was slightly ajar as he looked back and forth between his two cardinal mates. He rubbed his beak against the branch he was perched on.

"You know, cardinals mate for life," I said. "Three isn't a normal number for birds."

My mom nodded.

"So . . . do you think Grandpa John's a polygamist now?"

She laughed. She turned back to me, smiling. She looked healthier, happier, and at least momentarily without pain.

Grandma Mary flew out of sight, around the corner of the house, followed closely by the other two.

We watched them fly off. "That never gets old," my mom said.

I nodded.

She rolled to her other side slowly, then let her head sink into the pillow. As she closed her eyes, she said, "You know, maybe we should change up the birdseed out there. Alice is looking a little chunky."

# REDISCOVERING

## BIRDS

I've played a handful of different roles in my relatively short career as an actor. I've been a French aristocrat, a jellyfish, a heroin-addicted pornographer, a Roman centurion, a cat burglar, Pfizer trainee #1. At a summer theater program, I once played a pair of haunted cowboy boots.

Most of all, though, I've enjoyed getting to play America's most beloved pedophile.

The role of Ezra Fitz—despite the creep factor and the obvious ethical issues of dating a minor who happens to be one of my students—has been an incredible learning experience. I've played the part for seven years now, longer than any other role I've had, and I've grown substantially as an actor and as a person during my time as Ezra.

The first few seasons were a wild ride. I strapped in and hoped to God that I wouldn't fall off. The show turned out to be a hit—I was even getting recognized on the street. The whole experience was exciting and surreal, and every day was something new. I felt like I'd really made it.

But, as with everything, after a few seasons, the newness began to fade a little. I love my castmates and the crew—they are some of my favorite people on earth—but there were days on set when I counted down the hours until I could clock out and head home to see my girlfriend and play with my dogs. There were days when the job felt like a have-to instead of a get-to.

I knew I was in danger of becoming jaded. I was beginning to act like what Dustin Diamond might have called a "douche nozzle." I knew that I needed to shake the feeling off posthaste or I was going to start losing friends.

Nobody wants to hang out with a douche nozzle.

It was winter. Or the Los Angeles version of winter, elsewhere called "autumn." We were on break from filming, and I was going on a ski trip—a welcome chance to duck out of town for a few days and clear my head.

Every year since we graduated, a big group of my college friends and I have rented a cabin up in Big Bear Lake, a small town in the mountains about two hours northeast of LA. I studied acting at the Carnegie Mellon School of Drama, and I'm still close with a lot of my classmates. It's a tight-knit group, and the annual ski trip is a lot like a mafia summit—except instead of checking on business and figuring out whose knee-caps to break, the major goals are skiing and inebriation.

That year, we'd rented a cabin that could comfortably sleep six. There were two dozen of us, but we'd all gone to school together, so we were used to sharing beds.

The real problem was that it was only mid-December. We'd scheduled the trip a bit early that year, thinking nothing of the suspiciously low rental prices. There wasn't much snow yet. In fact, I'm pretty sure the only powder on the mountain was man-made. There were just two runs open in the entire resort: a bunny run for beginners, and a longer, intermediate-level blue.

The first day, we said screw it and decided to ski anyway. It was shorts and T-shirt weather on the mountain, not a cloud in the sky. The snow was the consistency of a Slurpee.

My friend Jack had never skied before, so I skied down the bunny slope with him a few times to help him with the basics. He got the hang of it pretty quickly, and after four or five times down, Jack decided he wanted to try his luck on the more difficult blue.

About a hundred yards into the run, Jack skidded over a rough patch of snow and went down. Hard. He reached out to catch himself and broke his arm—really shattered it.

I was above him on the mountain and didn't see him wipe out. I came around a bend to find several of my Carnegie compatriots huddled around him. At first I thought he was more shaken than hurt. But then Jack lifted his arm—it was bent at an unnatural angle: something was very wrong.

Jack had to be taken down the mountain in a paramedic snowmobile, and then we drove him to the emergency room in town.

In the ER, an unhygienically musky doctor came up to us. "What seems to be the problem here? Got a hurt arm?" he asked.

Before Jack could respond, the doctor reached out, grabbed his arm, and gave it a hard squeeze, shaking it up and down. Jack screamed and jerked his arm back. The doctor whistled. "That's definitely broken," he said.

"Yeah, you think?" Jack spat back.

For future reference: people with broken arms don't like having them squeezed and shaken. Just so you know.

Eventually a different doctor splinted Jack's arm and loaded him up with enough pain meds to knock out a small elephant. I offered to drive him back to LA, but Jack was a total champ and said he wanted to stay the rest of the weekend with us.

Unsurprisingly, the next morning nobody felt like skiing.

While we all tried to figure out what to do, my buddies Nick and Frank, both from New Jersey, both of Italian descent, made us all a massive breakfast. Nick and Frank are always the chefs on these trips. They never ski. They just come to hang out, drink, and cook, like the Italian grandmothers they secretly are.

My girlfriend Sophia and I loaded up our plates with eggs and pancakes and Italian sausages, and sat down at the breakfast table to feast.

Sophia and I have been together for six years, the longest I've been with anyone. We went to college together but didn't start dating until we'd both moved to Los Angeles. She has the looks of Audrey Hepburn and the comedic timing of Buster Keaton. She's also an exceptional photographer and artist.

One of our group, a friend from Carnegie we all call Wiggy, shuffled into the kitchen, half asleep, carrying an electric guitar and an amp. He was wearing boxers and an American flag T-shirt with the sleeves cut off. He grunted good morning to no one in particular and sat down on top of the table. He leaned over to plug in the amp and then proceeded to strum out a series of death metal arpeggios.

I reached over and unplugged the amp. Wiggy continued to play as if nothing had changed.

After breakfast, I took a couple of people into town to the grocery store. We needed to stock up on provisions since we weren't going back out on the slopes. Mostly I think we were getting beer for a little day drinking. Maybe marshmallows and chocolate bars for s'mores.

On the drive to town, I started feeling irritable. The weekend was beginning to seem like a total waste. It wasn't my friends' fault. It was me.

I'd been craving activity—something to take my mind off everything. Instead, I found myself once again worrying about my work and the ever-lengthening to-do list I'd left back in Los Angeles.

Driving into town, to the right of the car, there was a massive, shimmering body of water. Big Bear Lake is named for a lake, after all. The late-morning light glittered beckoningly off the surface of the water.

Sitting shotgun was a guy named Walter—a childhood friend of my CMU buddy John. We'd just met the day before. He was one of the only people on the trip who hadn't gone to Carnegie—he may well have been the only person there who hadn't studied theater or taken an acting class. For most of the drive he'd been looking out the window, which I assumed was because he was new to the group.

Walter was on the lake-side of the car, and as we drove along, I glanced over to look out at the water. Looking over, I could see that he was focused intently on an object floating on the lake.

I craned my neck forward to look past him. Close to the shore was a duck, floating serenely on the glittering blue. It had a low, sleek profile, and a thin bill. Not your normal duck profile, if that's the kind of thing you pay attention to.

Something about that bird drew me in. For a moment, I was at a loss. I kept driving in silence. A word lodged somewhere in the depths of my brain bubbled up into consciousness: *merganser.*

That's what it was, a type of duck called a merganser.

I braked for a stop sign, then drove on. But I couldn't get the bird out of my head. I looked at Walter. He'd definitely seen that duck. But did he know what it was?

"Merganser," I mumbled. There was a good chance he'd have no idea what I was talking about.

Walter looked over. A big smile spread across his face. "Yeah, dude. That was a hooded merganser!"

"Wait, for real?" I said. "How'd you know what that was?"

Turns out Walter, who'd grown up in Texas, had been a birder since he was a little kid.

I was a birder when I was a kid, too. I just hadn't thought about it in a really long time.

When I was younger—way younger, like back before elementary school—I loved looking at birds. It was one of my childhood passions. Right up there with Pogs and poop jokes.

I was born in Heidelberg, Germany. My parents were both in the U.S. military, and they were stationed there when I was a baby. When I was three years old, they got called back state-side, so we moved from Germany to Springfield, Virginia.

Our first home back in the States was a red-brick town house with forest-green shutters. It was a picture-perfect middle-class suburban home. I had a best friend who lived three doors down, and my sister's best friend lived next door. It was a safe place for kids to play out front in the street. One time some high-schoolers had a knife fight on a basketball court nearby and the cops showed up, but nothing else exciting ever happened.

Behind our house, a path led across a little creek to a playground in the woods. There were swings, a slide, a merry-go-round. And beyond all that, the forest stretched out endlessly.

There were squirrels and deer and foxes. Crawfish in the stream. And lots and lots of birds. I'd chase the robins that were perched on the ground. I don't know what I would have done if I'd ever caught one. But I liked following them. I wanted to get as close as possible.

At some point it occurred to me that instead of going out and chasing them, I could get the birds to come to me.

I went through the trash at home and pulled out all the empty plastic soda bottles. I cut holes in the sides and filled them with birdseed. I then tied strings around the necks of the bottles, and hung them from low-hanging branches in our backyard. For neighbors walking by, it must've looked like some low-budget human sacrifice cult. The whole setup was pretty *Blair Witch*-y.

Once the feeders were hanging from the trees, I went up to my bedroom on the second floor and waited for the birds to arrive. I had a cheap pair of binoculars with plastic lenses, and over the coming weeks I'd patiently focus them on the nuthatches, woodpeckers, sparrows, and goldfinches that came in to feed. It was like *Rear Window*, except without any murder. Unless you count the murder of crows.

Sorry. That was just—I'm sorry.

The point is, I really liked birds. I had notebooks full of drawings of them that I copied out of an Audubon field guide. And in second grade, I once threw a tantrum when my science project group wanted to build a model volcano instead of a bird feeder.

But then I graduated to middle school. Puberty happened, as it does to many people. I became far more self-conscious and felt a strong need to fit in with the other kids. Birding is often a solitary pursuit. It's not something you need to share with others. For as much joy as it brought me, I was afraid it would come across as weird, outsider behavior.

Also, middle-schoolers think about sex a lot: like, all the time. To my thirteen-year-old mind, birding was the equivalent of a vow of chastity. I couldn't risk it, so I very willfully set birds aside.

There's a book I read recently that reminds me of my middle school experience. Before J. M. Barrie wrote *Peter and Wendy*—the classic tale of Peter Pan and Captain Hook and the wonders of Neverland—he wrote a book called *The Little White Bird*. This book is the first time Barrie ever wrote about a boy named Peter Pan. Before there was a Neverland, before there were pirates or mermaids, there was just a little boy locked in a park at night after the gates had closed.

Barrie talks in the book about how all children used to be

birds: "They are naturally a little wild during the first few weeks, and very itchy at the shoulders, where their wings used to be." Children only become fully human when they forget how to fly. And forgetting how to fly is easy. It just takes doubt. The moment you first doubt whether or not you can fly is the moment you lose the gift of flight forever. The moment when you cease to be a bird and become a human, destined to grow old and dull and unimaginative.

In my adolescence, I took this odd interest I had, and I hid it. Buried it. I was afraid of getting picked on, of getting made fun of by the opposite sex, by anyone really. It was easier to be normal and try to fit in—and wash my face three times a day to prevent breakouts. As long as I tried to be like everyone else—as long as I tried to look normal—I had a chance at being cool. And it's embarrassing to admit it, but being cool meant a lot to me. I wanted to be friends with everyone. Birding seemed like the opposite of all that. If anything, it just seemed like a way to be friends with old people. And everyone in middle school knows that old people aren't cool.

When high school rolled around, I'd forgotten that I'd ever even liked birds in the first place. My attention and interests were elsewhere. I switched from a public middle school to a private high school called Georgetown Prep. I wasn't used to the rigorous academics, and I had to work a lot harder in class.

In high school I also discovered acting, which was a whole new creative outlet for me. I spent all of my free time in Figge, the school's theater building. I would often set up a table in the middle of the stage to do my homework, the auditorium otherwise empty. Sometimes the janitor would kick me out—I would walk around the building and sneak back in.

Now, sitting in the car in Big Bear, looking at the hooded merganser, I felt a familiar excitement rising in my chest, a connection to my childhood—back to when I'd stared out my bedroom window, learning the names of the birds that were eating from the bird feeders I'd made.

I had forgotten that just looking at birds—simply watching them, observing their idiosyncratic behaviors and colorful beauty—could bring me such joy. I felt inspired, light, and totally in touch with a part of me that had been lying dormant for almost fifteen years.

"What the hell is a merganser?" someone said from the backseat.

I looked at Walter: "You want to tell him?"

Walter tried to downplay it. "It's a kind of duck," he said.

I suddenly felt a flash of defiance—not at Walter, but at the entire situation. I'd stopped birding as a child because I'd felt judged by my peers. Here I was, twenty-five years old, an adult, and I was feeling embarrassed by birds again? If I didn't stand up for myself now, when the hell was I going to start?

I half shouted, "It's not just a duck!" I had no idea where I was going with this, but I had to set the record straight. "It's got a serrated bill! It's a fucking awesome duck!"

Yeah, that'd show them. That would make them understand.

From the backseat, a bored voice said, "Whatever," and then went back to what they'd been talking about before the merganser interlude.

When we got back to the cabin with provisions an hour later people were getting antsy. It was downright balmy outside—a ridiculous, global warming–induced seventy degrees. Someone suggested to the group that, since we couldn't ski, we all go for a hike along Big Bear Lake.

A handful of people wanted to stay back to get drunk and eat marshmallows, and Wiggy was still strumming his unplugged guitar, but the rest of us piled into a couple of cars and drove back down to the lake. We parked near a bridge.

As we were getting out of the cars, putting on sunscreen, I noticed that Walter had a small pair of binoculars hanging around his neck.

"Do you always have those around?" I asked.

"Yeah. Actually, I keep them in the glove compartment of my car," he said. "It might be crazy, but you never know. I've seen a lot of birds in places I wouldn't have expected to find them."

The group set off, tromping around the lake. I was suddenly aware again of the world in a different but oddly familiar way. Birds were outlined in silhouette out on the water. They were chirping overhead in the trees and in the bushes along the shore. I was paying attention to every sound.

I wasn't in my head, worrying about work, or thinking about how I needed to watch what I ate over the holidays. It might sound like some hippie California nonsense, but I felt very, very present.

A flock of birds fluttered between trees off to the side of the trail, gorging themselves on tiny red berries. Walter passed me his binoculars. I raised them to my eyes and adjusted the focus knob with my index finger, trying to get a bird to come into view.

The birds were moving targets, and I was out of practice. I lowered the binoculars and looked for them again. I could hear them: their call a single high-pitched note, barely noticeable unless you were listening for it.

Suddenly there was a flurry of wings as one hovered to snatch a berry. I quickly raised the binoculars and adjusted the focus: a little brown crest, a black mask, a dab of yellow at the end of the bird's tail. Very sleek, very elegant. A cedar waxwing.

I made a mental note to invest in a pair of binoculars when I got back to Los Angeles.

In the bushes along the shore, another bird called—it sounded like the avian version of an old-timey phone ring. I could swear I'd heard that call before, but I couldn't place it.

"That's a red-winged blackbird," Walter said, as it flew out and landed in the branches at the top of the bush. It was a glossy black, with red and yellow epaulettes on its wings.

Farther along, coots were paddling close to shore. We scanned the lake—no sign of that merganser. I noticed a bird twisting its way up a tree. A downy woodpecker? It spiraled back around the trunk, coming into view. Not a woodpecker after all, but a white-breasted nuthatch.

It was the same type of nuthatch that had come in to the feeders I'd set up in my backyard in Virginia when I was a kid. Here I was, wandering around a lake in California, the same boy that used to play in the woods, chasing robins.

In the far distance, Sophia and my friend Michele were skipping stones, trying to hit a floating log. The rest of the group was out of sight down the path.

I didn't mind being left behind—it was like I'd found a key to a room that hadn't been opened for years, and I was just beginning to explore what was under all the dust that had accumulated. It was slow work, but I was ecstatic. Yes, that's the word. Ecstatic. It was like reconnecting with a long-lost friend. I couldn't stop smiling.

Walter pointed out birds as we walked along. A lot of them were different from the ones I'd grown up with. I had a lot to learn, and a lot to relearn. There was a childlike sense of wonder to the whole experience: I was a birder again.

Of course, the trip had to come to an end. As I drove back to Los Angeles at the end of the long weekend, there was a lump in my throat. My mind kept jumping back to the merganser, and to all the other birds we'd spotted around the lake. I didn't know when I'd get another chance to go birding like that again.

Later that week, I found myself back on the Warner Bros. lot, wandering past the sound stages where *Pretty Little Liars* is filmed. The show was on hiatus, but I had a casting session for a horror film.

Driving onto the lot, I was feeling irritable again. I wanted to be back in the mountains. And just being in the physical location of where I work made me a little anxious—for something different, for something more. Looking to the mountains in the distance, I felt completely cut off from nature.

I parked and got out of the car. Just then, a pair of swallows darted by, spiraling over and under each other as they shot up into the sky and vanished overhead. I was stunned. I stood there in awe, trying to see where the birds had disappeared to.

An assistant with a clipboard walked up. "Everything okay?" he asked.

"Yeah," I said, still looking up at the sky. "Just trying to see where those swallows went."

The assistant scratched his head. "I know there are a couple of birds that live up in the WB sign," he said, pointing toward Stage 16.

Right above the load-in doors on the soundstage, the iconic WB sign beamed out over the lot. Nestled in the shade below the *W*, a nest made of mud clung to the side of the sign.

"That's it!" I said. "Those are cliff swallows."

I smiled. It felt good to be back. I'd left the mountains behind, but birds—birds are everywhere. I just hadn't been looking for them.

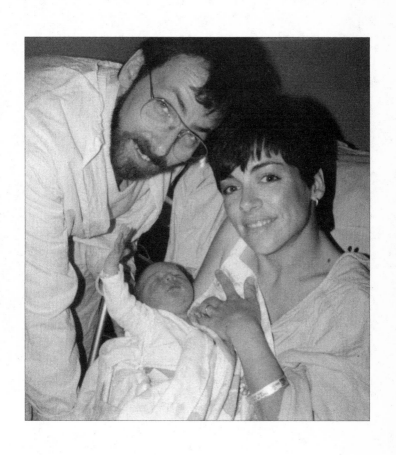

## H IS FOR

## MR. HAWKINS

They say that second children are easy to raise. After the stress and steep learning curve of the firstborn child, kid number two is supposed to be a breeze.

This was not the case in my family. My big sister Sarah was an easy child, practically angelic. You could give her a book, and she'd sit quietly, entertaining herself, for hours.

I was—as my dear aunt Jules often tells me—a nightmare.

I was a master of tantrums, a great shitter of diapers, and a consummate destroyer of fine china. Then one day I started talking, and the tantrums stopped. To hear my parents tell it, it was all very sudden. The moment I learned to communicate, I stopped lashing out.

I was still a terror, just in different, subtler ways.

We went through a steady stream of babysitters. None of them lasted that long. One time, while my parents were out on a date, trying to remove themselves from the stress of childcare for a few precious hours, our babysitter asked us if we wanted to play hide-and-seek.

This was very exciting for me except for one slight hang-up: I was terrible at hide-and-seek. I was four at the time, and I had a four-year-old's perception of good hiding spots. I hid under the dining table. Sarah found me. I tried hiding behind the couch. She found me again. There is just no winning at hide-and-seek when you are four and your older sister is seven.

That's when it occurred to me: the perfect hiding spot. There was one place where they'd never think to look.

I waited until the babysitter was "it." As she began her slow count to thirty, I watched Sarah sneak up the stairs toward our parents' bathroom. So that's where she'd been hiding.

I turned the opposite way and snuck out the front door, around the side of the house, and into the woods. Brilliant, I thought. They'd never find me in the woods at night.

I mentioned earlier that our house backed up to a forest. The jump from manicured suburbs to wilderness was sudden and thrilling. There was a trail that started just behind our house. Twenty paces in and you were plunged into darkness. The temperature fell, and the sounds of birds enveloped you. The path was edged with moss and Virginia creeper, and it curved its way through the trees for what felt like miles.

My parents would let my sister and me play in the woods on our own. My dad would give us an old Timex watch, and tell us when to be home. The game was to see how far we could get into the forest and still make it back in time for dinner. We'd bushwhack through the undergrowth, hop across stone bridges.

From time to time, we'd pass a playground or a backyard, but gradually those started to disappear. Bit by bit, the neighborhood dissolved around us and we forgot where we were. The path forked again and again, branching out into the woods like blood vessels. Walking along, turning left then right then left again, I felt like I could get lost in those woods for days.

There was a creek that ran through the forest. Ferns lined its edges, and small herds of deer would stop to drink. When my sister and I had friends over, we would all go down to the creek to catch crawfish. One of our friends sometimes brought a net, but the rest of us just used our hands. We never ate the crawfish we caught; the goal was to catch the biggest and to make sure that everyone else saw how big it was before you threw it back into the water.

The best crawfish lived in the spots where the creek got its widest, where the water slowed to a crawl. We would wade in and lift up the biggest rocks we could. In the cloud of dust and leaf litter that got stirred up under the rocks, we could usually find one or two crawfish.

The woods were our second home. And as far as I was concerned, I was Robinson Crusoe.


That night, playing hide-and-seek, I started walking down the usual path, but it was extremely dark outside. Still, I was riding the high of having potentially won a round of hide-and-seek, and I wasn't about to turn back now. I kept on walking.

After walking about a mile, the path sloped up. I followed it until it spit me out on the side of a busy street. As I walked along the road, a four-year-old marching proudly in his Batman pajamas, a white SUV slowed down and pulled up beside me. The window rolled down to reveal a woman about my mother's age.

"Are you lost, honey? Do you need help?" she said.

I shook my head. "No thanks!"

"Are you sure?"

"I'm playing hide-and-seek," I said, smiling.

She let out a nervous laugh. "I'll bet you're winning."

"I am!"

"Listen, you should probably head back. I'm sure your parents are worried sick about you. Can I give you a ride home?"

"I'm not allowed to ride in the car with strangers," I said.

"Good point." She put the car in park and got out. "Come on," she said, reaching out her hand to take mine. "Let's walk."

I told her my address, and we walked home together. When I opened my front door, the first thing I saw was my dad pacing back and forth. Our babysitter had called the restaurant— this was before cellphones—to tell my parents that I'd gone missing. When he saw me, he let out a cry. I'd never heard my dad make that sound. He lifted me up in his arms, a wave of emotion flooding his face, and held me against his chest. He walked me into the living room, where my mom was sitting on the couch with the babysitter, who was crying into her hands.

"Ian, where on earth have you been?" my mom asked.

I smiled. "I won the game."

After that, I wasn't allowed to go into the woods on my

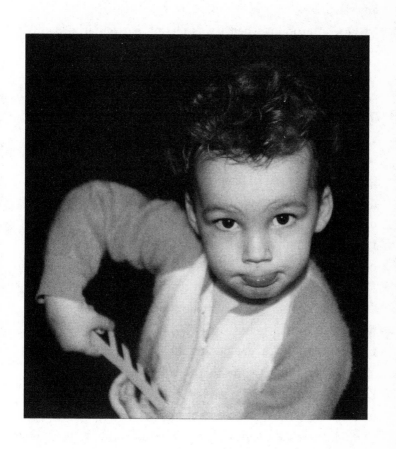

own for a while. But it soon became clear that it wasn't a good idea for me to remain indoors, either. I was a hyperactive kid, like I said, and if I didn't have an outlet for all of my energy, things would get broken and nobody in the house would get any sleep.

One afternoon, when I was feeling particularly rowdy, my dad volunteered to go tire me out. I was up in my room, spinning in circles. My dad stood at the bottom of the staircase and called up: "Ian, do you want to come exploring with me?"

I raced down the stairs, threw some shoes on, and we were off. My dad and I hiked around the woods for the better part of the afternoon. I was so happy to be back outside. I showed my dad all of my favorite crawfish spots, and he told me about the different types of trees we were walking by. When I got home, I was exhausted. I slept soundly that night. And so did my parents.

They had found a way to get rid of my excess energy.

My dad and I went exploring pretty often after he'd get home from work. I, being your average four-year-old, could not pronounce the word "explore," though. So we went on 'splores.

It was on these 'splores that I first noticed birds. I mean, I knew what birds were, I wasn't a complete shut-in. I'd seen the cardinals in our backyard and heard my mom's stories about them. I'd smelled the deathly musk of pigeons outside of the natural history museum in DC. But this was the first time that I ever became aware of their variety, of their nesting habits, their flight patterns, and their distinct, vibrating calls echoing through the woods.

My dad seemed to know all about them. We'd hear a rus-

tling in the trees, and he'd point up and say, "That's a crow, Ian."
I'd laugh—because the word sounded funny to my ears—and
then I'd try to mimic its call.

I had wanted things before: the previous Christmas, I had
really wanted light-up sneakers. So desire was not a new con-
cept to me.

But this was the first time I remember wanting to understand something. I wanted to know everything there was to
know about birds. I wanted to devour them with my mind and
absorb all of their secrets. The secret of flight, how to perch,
what worms tasted like, why they never had to pee . . . I wanted
to know it all.

There was one bird in particular that I absolutely loved. I
asked my dad what kind of bird it was, and he said it was a hawk.
So, naturally, I named him Mr. Hawkins.

Every time we went out 'sploring, I would run ahead of my
dad into the woods to see my new friend. Mr. Hawkins would
always stare at me with a slightly surprised and cautious look
on his face. At the time, I always thought that he was pretending not to remember me, so I would play along and call out to
remind him, "Mr. Hawkins! It's me, Ian!"

In retrospect, I now realize that the look on Mr. Hawkins's
face was one of deliberation: Do I flee from this screaming
child or try to somehow eat him?

When I was in the second grade, we moved from Springfield
to Herndon, an even smaller town, which was nestled in the
shadow of Dulles airport. A lot of the public schools in northern
Virginia have the exact same floor plan, so the transition to a

new school wasn't particularly difficult, at least spatially. What I was worried about was saying goodbye to 'splores with my dad.

Despite its proximity to both airplanes and politicians, Herndon still felt rural. My new home was within walking distance of Trailside Park, a perfect place for new and exciting adventures.

Every day after school I would rush home, grab my binoculars, and my dad and I would wander off to the park to look for birds. It turned out there was a hawk that lived in the Herndon park, too. I was convinced that it was Mr. Hawkins, and I couldn't believe his loyalty—he had moved all the way across the county to be with us.

Some friends just last forever, you know.

It was clear to my dad that birds were becoming a passion of mine. One day—I think I was about six—my dad took me into his study. He pulled an old book off his shelves and handed it to me.

"I thought this might help," he said, smiling down at me.

The book was significantly older than I was. The cover was made of fake leather. The white lettering along the spine cracked and illegible. The corners of the pages were all bent with age and humidity. I opened the book and turned to the title page: *The Audubon Society: Field Guide to North American Birds.*

I flipped to a random page. There were row upon row of photographs. In each photograph, a different bird. Birds I'd never seen before. Birds I'd never imagined could exist. Names I couldn't even dream of pronouncing. The book was bursting with information.

I thanked my dad and hugged his knees—I was shorter then. I looked up at him and asked, "Is Mr. Hawkins in here?"

He took the book from my hands and flipped through the pages pensively for a few moments. Then his face relaxed into a grin. He handed the book back to me and pointed to one of the pictures on the page. It was a red-tailed hawk.

I giggled. "His tail *is* red!" I cried, unable to control my glee.

I didn't sleep that night. My mom and dad came by to check on me before going to bed, and I turned off the light and pretended to be sleeping. But as soon as they left, the light was back on and the book was open. There was a whole world of birds out there for me to explore.

The next time we went to Trailside Park, I brought the bird book with me. When I saw Mr. Hawkins perched high up on a branch that day, I opened up the book to the earmarked page with the red-tailed hawk on it and held it up for him to see.

"Mr. Hawkins!" I shouted, "Look! They took your picture. It's you!"

Mr. Hawkins looked down at me, startled, and promptly flew away. My dad told me that Mr. Hawkins was probably just shy and didn't like looking at his own picture.

The Audubon guide was the second book I had ever fallen in love with. The first was *The Velveteen Rabbit*, a copy of which I carried everywhere with me for months. I read it again and again, pressing my finger up against the rabbit's nose, letting him know that I had believed he was real all along.

My dad and I often ran across a little brown rabbit in the woods. I was convinced that it was the Velveteen Rabbit come to life. Every time we saw it, I would unsuccessfully attempt to suppress a gasp, and my finger would shoot out, pointing at the terrified bunny in our path. My dad explained to me that this wasn't the Velveteen Rabbit from the book—it was our Velveteen Rabbit, and we could name him whatever we wanted.

We settled on Sir Hopsalot.

One day in the woods near our house I saw Sir Hopsalot sitting in a field. He was munching on some tall grass and didn't seem to notice my dad and me walking toward him.

My dad stayed behind as I slowly, stealthily crept toward the rabbit. I could see his whiskers twitching with each bite he took. He must have realized I was nearby, because he sat up on his hind legs, alert, his nose twitching. His ears twisted around like a satellite dish.

I had never been this close to a wild animal before. He was beautiful. If I could just get a little closer, I knew that I could reach out and pet him. Just a little tiny bit closer.

Sir Hopsalot pricked his ears up, and became very still. He raised his head and looked at me. I knew it: he was finally ready to say hello.

I took another cautious step forward.

There was a soft thud as Mr. Hawkins slammed into Sir Hopsalot.

Talons ripped open the rabbit's soft belly, spilling its guts out across the field of grass and clover. Wings outstretched, the hawk throttled the rabbit against the ground, making sure it was dead.

I stood there, stunned, as Mr. Hawkins swiveled his head up from his prey and looked me in the eye, daring me to take one more step.

The hawk took off, Sir Hopsalot a deflated balloon of red fur clutched in its talons.

My dad must have carried me back after that, because I don't remember walking home. I was too busy crying.

From then on, I was always decidedly curt—cold, even—when I greeted Mr. Hawkins in the woods. I was scarred. It was the most brutal thing I'd ever seen.

But I did learn a valuable life lesson that day: just because you're friends with two people doesn't mean they'll get along.

# MY INNER
# ANIMAL

I'd been called in to audition for the role of a Holocaust survivor.

The idea of auditioning for a part like this gave me more stress than usual. There are certain roles where when you portray them, you aren't just a person, you're a stand-in for an entire people. I felt like I could never possibly do justice to the character.

The week before the audition, I spent six hours a day prepping. Every morning, I'd wake up, and read through the scene again, and feel like I had to start over from scratch. I couldn't get a foothold on the character.

I tried out half a dozen different accents—and a physicality for each one—and none of them seemed to fit. Around day three, I stopped drinking water, hoping that doing so might give my throat the sort of rasp I imagined the character might have.

My studio apartment had shag carpeting, and I was pacing back and forth so much every day that I was beginning to wear tracks in it.

I was feeling tired and weak, and more than once I thought about calling my agent and telling him to call off the audition. I just couldn't do it, I wanted to say.

I'd forgotten that I'd stopped drinking water, and one morning, as I was pacing, I felt the room begin to spin around me— once, twice, then a third time. I reached out to grab the back of a chair to steady myself.

When the room finally came to rest, I bent my knees to make sure they still worked.

They wobbled a little. My legs felt weak, fluid almost.

I felt like I was out on the ocean, floating adrift. I felt like a jellyfish.

I hadn't felt that sensation in years, but it was undeniable. Believe me when I say I know exactly what it feels like to be a jellyfish: there was a period in my life where I spent eight hours a day, every day—for months—pretending to be one.

My dad drove me up to Pittsburgh for my first year of college. I was leaving the nest for the first time, and though leaving behind the world I'd grown up in saddened me, I was getting a chance to pursue the one thing in the world I really wanted to do. I was about to begin to study acting at the Carnegie Mellon School of Drama.

Even with all the excitement, it was more difficult to say goodbye than I expected. My parents had gotten divorced the year before, and my mom was selling the house in Herndon that I'd grown up in. When I left for college, it was already on the market, and I knew that when I came back to visit for Thanksgiving, it would be to an entirely different home.

When my dad and I arrived in Pittsburgh, we immediately went to my freshman dorm to get moved in. That year I lived in an all-male dorm called Hamerschlag. My new roommate, Joe, who was a music major, also happened to be there, moving in at the same time.

Joe was from South Africa, by way of Baltimore. He had a big mop of curly hair, thick-rimmed glasses, and he was virtually inseparable from his cherry-red electric guitar.

I remember lying in bed that first night, thinking about this new life I was about to embark upon. It's bizarre being plopped into a new living situation with a stranger for a whole year. Joe and I started talking to each other in the dark, talking about ourselves, seeing how we got along. At some point, he stopped responding.

I looked over: he had fallen asleep in child's pose—a position he ended up sleeping in often. I still don't understand how he was able to fall asleep with his butt in the air. What was not so cute, though, was that he often liked to sleep naked.

That first year at CMU was a blast, but it was also a lot of work. The School of Drama puts its students through the ringer. It's an acting conservatory, so we didn't have any classes that weren't theater-related. We'd spend five days a week, from 7:00 A.M. to 11:00 P.M., studying acting and building sets for the school's plays. Sunup till way after sundown. Then, on

Saturdays, we'd regularly have an additional half day of set-building.

Fall semester was a whirlwind, and looking back, a lot of it is a blur. There were so many new people to meet, a whole new city to explore, and classes were more than a full-time commitment. I had been the only person from my all-boys Catholic high school to pursue acting in college, and I was suddenly surrounded by some of the most talented people I'd ever met. It was intimidating. But over the course of four years of working with the same people, that sense of intimidation—and the natural competition between students—gave way to camaraderie and friendship. Some of my best friends to this day I met during those four years at Carnegie.

We had a month off for Christmas, so I went back to stay with my mom in Virginia. She'd moved into a new two-bedroom apartment, and since my sister was also home for the break, I slept in a little loft that was actually the laundry room.

While I was back home, I met up with a few of my closest childhood friends. We all had one foot in our old Virginia high-school world, and all the shared experiences of that time, and one foot in our college worlds, on the verge of new, independent lives. We weren't twenty-one yet, so we were still in this odd hang-out limbo. We'd play basketball at the Y until it closed, then go to Chipotle. After that, we'd drink at someone's house.

One night, we were all over at my friend Chris's house. There were four or five of us hanging out, shooting the shit, comparing notes on college, bragging about how much we'd partied and the girls we'd met. My other friends all seemed to be headed toward careers in business or medicine or the military.

The guys asked what I was up to. I took a swig of my beer. "I've been doing a lot of physical stuff this semester. It's called Viewpoints. Basically, it's about how you walk around a room and the different ways you can interact with the architecture."

Good. I'd used some big words—I'd even said the word "architecture"—so nobody could deny that I was doing important things.

"That's it?" Chris asked. "You've been learning how to walk around a room?"

"Well, that's not the only thing I'm doing. I have voice class, and speech class, and acting—"

"Voice and speech are two different classes?"

I was starting to feel judged.

"Yeah, speech is all about accents and dialects. This year we're learning Standard American. Next year we learn General American . . ." I trailed off as I realized everyone's eyes had glazed over.

"Anyway, yeah," I said.

Matt tried to be nice: "Have anything fun coming up next semester?"

I took a sip of beer and sighed. "Next semester they want me to figure out what kind of animal I am."

For a while nobody said anything. Then everyone started laughing. Matt grinned. "So, you're in kindergarten."


The first week back after the holiday break, our professors stood us up at the front of the classroom, one by one, and assigned us each an animal.

"Adam, you're a bear."

"Vicki, definitely a catfish."

"Shunan, dear God, could you be more of a penguin?"

When it was my turn, I walked up to the front of the room. The professors put their heads together and whispered. I put my hands behind my back, trying to loosen up my shoulders. After a moment, one of the professors laughed a little, and they all turned back to face me.

"You exude false confidence," one of them said. "Like a mouse with a Napoleon complex." The two other professors nodded in agreement. Behind them, one of my classmates snorted.

The professor continued, "You need to be the complete opposite: an animal that has no ego, no sense of self."

He sat back in his chair and crossed his arms. For a few moments nobody spoke. Then he squinted and leaned forward—"Any ideas?"

I was—to put it lightly—hurt. This assessment of my outward demeanor was tough to stomach. I stood there, trying to shake off what the professor had said, but it was affecting me more than I wanted to admit. Definitely more than I wanted my classmates to see.

I tried to laugh it off. "What, like a jellyfish?" I joked.

The teacher who had issued the critique raised his eyebrows. "Exactly," he said. "You'll be a jellyfish."

We were assigned our animals on a Friday. We were to present them the following Monday. And by "present" I mean act out in front of the class.

That weekend, a number of my classmates went to the Pittsburgh Zoo to research their animals. They wanted to observe their behavior and movement firsthand.

Meanwhile, I did what I had learned to do in high school for research projects: I went to the library.

I wandered into the Carnegie Library and found a librarian.

"Hi there," I said. "Do you have any books on jellyfish?"

"Is this for a research project?" she asked.

"Yes—I have to be one."

She gave me an odd look but didn't press for an explanation.

On Sunday I locked myself in my dorm room and read through all the books I'd checked out. I watched the few jellyfish clips I could find online—it was still the early days of YouTube.

After exhaustive research, I stood in front of the full-length mirror on the back of the door to the room and did all the things that a human does when they're pretending to be a jellyfish.

I hunched my shoulders forward and let my arms dangle like tentacles. I pulsed my body, as if propelling myself through an invisible ocean. I tried to ride the ebb and flow of the land-locked Pittsburgh tide.

I looked at myself in the mirror—I felt like a crazy person.

I kept at it, though. An hour went by. I continued to wriggle my body in shallow, jellyfish-like convulsions.

A second hour went by, and I looked down at my feet, tethered to the ground, holding me back—

Suddenly, the secret to imitating a jellyfish struck me.

The secret to being a great jellyfish—and this is important—it's all in the ankles.

I wobbled my ankles back and forth, letting the momentum wiggle up to my hips. I pushed up on the balls of my feet, heels elevated slightly off the ground, then slowly drifted back down.

Proud of my discovery, proud of how great my jellyfish performance would be, I stood there in front of the mirror and continued to bend my ankles. I felt sure I was bending them just like a jellyfish would.

All of a sudden, Joe was standing where the mirror had just been. I was wearing my skintight drama-school-issued black unitard, and writhing up and down.

"Uh, hey Joe. Just rehearsing for class."

"Don't mind me. What're you working on?"

"You know, Animal Projects . . ."

Joe didn't say anything.

"I'm a jellyfish."

Joe was unfazed. He sat down on his bed and pulled out his electric guitar.

"Keep doing your thing," he said. He plucked at the strings, letting them vibrate in a gentle and meditative deep-sea sort of way. "I'm just going to play us some jellyfish music."

His face took on the expression one gets when deep in prayer. To this day, he's one of the only people I know who sees music as not simply something to listen and dance to, but as a form of communion with something greater.


Monday came, and I walked into the drama building with more confidence than ever before. When it was my turn to present, I strode up to the front of the classroom. I cleared my mind and then focused on my ankles. I whispered to myself, "Mind of a jellyfish. Mind of a jellyfish."

I don't remember what happened next: All I know is that I was a jellyfish. I was born a jellyfish. I could not remember a day when I hadn't been a jellyfish.

After a minute or two of gelatinous pulsating, my professor politely asked me to stop. "Good work, Ian. Very specific," he said.

I smiled. This was one of the first real compliments I'd received in acting class at Carnegie.

"Really good start at your jellyfish," the professor went on. "Excited to see this develop over the next two months."


Animal Projects, it turned out, was not just a few days of research followed by a presentation. It was eight weeks of pretending to be a man-sized scyphozoan. It was the only thing we did in class.

One of the requirements of the project was to construct a costume, so the following weekend I took a bus down to the Waterfront, a strip of big-box stores along the Monongahela River. I had an idea, and I needed bedsheets.

I wandered into Bed Bath & Beyond. On a sales rack I found a set of fluorescent lime-green sheets on clearance. I don't think I'd ever seen a green jellyfish before, but I figured I could take some artistic license. And the sheets were the right price: extremely cheap.

Back in my dorm room, I cut long strips into the flat sheet and tied it around my shoulders. Neon-green fabric reached down to the floor around my body—these were my tentacles. I then took the fitted sheet and taped it over a hula hoop, which created a puffy, human-sized jellyfish bell. I put the sheet-covered hula hoop over my head, holding it up with my arms.

Looking down, I could only see one or two feet in any direction. I could barely make out anything through the sheet around me—the world was a fuzzy green blur. I couldn't make out the costume in the mirror, so I had no idea what I looked like, but it felt right.

I stood there, in the middle of the room, and I did my jelly-fish ankles. I felt the tentacles brush up against my legs, the green bell around my head drifting and floating through the air.

Joe said that I was the most realistic jellyfish he'd ever seen in Pittsburgh.

The next two months of class were a little lonely. I couldn't see much because of my costume, and I didn't interact with many of the other animals. Most of my classmates were terrestrial mammals, but I lived in the ocean. We weren't about to mess with the laws of nature.

Every morning, the professor would set aside a little spot for me to wiggle and jiggle and do my jelly-shaking thing. We called this spot "water," and I shared it with Vicki the catfish. Sometimes a penguin or two would jump in, but most of the other animals avoided it. We'd practice our animals, and the professor would walk around, adjusting postures, commenting on the way the gorillas grabbed at their food, reminding the big cats to be aware of their spinal cords.

I would float there, in my imaginary pool of water, counting my breaths—and remembering to lead with my ankles.

Weeks went by like this, which in jellyfish years is . . . a lot.

I spent that winter floating. Floating in the pond. But I also felt like I was floating in life, carried along by forces out of my control. College is about leaving home and growing up, but you're still a kid. And I felt bittersweet about leaving home, anyway.

A lot had changed in a matter of months. I wasn't homesick—I was actually glad to be out on my own. But there was this feeling, somewhere deep, that I'd left a part of me behind along the way.

It wasn't just that I couldn't go back to my old home anymore. There was a part of me that was no longer there. Or a part of me that was changing, transitioning from one set of circumstances to another.

Looking back on it now, I think the jellyfish may have had something to do with it. I felt trapped. I needed an outlet, and I spent my days physically constricted, only able to see my feet and the floor beneath me. Had I been assigned a different animal—a gorilla, or a tiger—I could have lashed out, roared, beat my chest. But I was a jellyfish, subject to the whims of the tides and of the people around me.

I see that my trajectory throughout my college years was borne along by those same tides. I made big decisions then that have affected my future, but I've also had my life determined in many ways by the decisions of others.

This is a big part of being human, and especially being an actor.

Animal Projects culminated in a three-hour event called "Watering Hole." The freshman class had been divided into three sections, and this was a chance for the entire class to come together and sniff and growl and love on one another as animals.

Unfortunately, I was still one of the only aquatic animals—and I couldn't see more than two feet in any direction.

For the first hour and a half, I floated around my lonely patch of ocean as my classmates scampered about. I could hear them playing and rolling around on the ground. At one point, a teacher announced that the "sun had set," and everyone pretended to go to sleep as their animal. Everyone except for me, because I was a goddamn jellyfish. The sun rose again, and the animals awoke with a series of deep-chested growls and loud roar-yawns.

I continued to bob slowly up and down.

Then things started to get tense. I could sense a change in the mood of the room. The animals that had played together earlier were getting more aggressive. The faculty sensed it, too, and one of the teachers—her name was Ingrid—shouted: "Predators, KILL!"

Loud and frantic screeching immediately filled the air. Somebody threw a chair against a wall—I flinched at the crash. Students were clawing at each other, shrieking, running around me. The room was filled with the sounds of carnage.

I continued to float, rising and falling from my ankles. When the room had quieted down, I angled my hula hoop up so that I could look around.

Most of the student-animals were dead, their bodies strewn about the room. The predators prowled about, letting out blood-curdling howls and roars as they sized each other up. The lions growled at the gorillas, who beat their chests with clenched fists in response.

And I just kept floating. Up. And down.

Then, like a hypnotist, Ingrid clapped her hands and announced that Watering Hole was over. We were humans again.


Years later, standing dizzy and dehydrated in my small apartment in LA—trying to figure out the physicality of a Holocaust survivor—I thought back to how I'd felt in my months as a jellyfish during that first year of college.

I became aware of my ankles again. I took a deep breath in and lifted up the heels of my feet, letting my body float a little.

I closed my eyes and ran through the lines in my head. I felt unmoored. Without a home. Adrift. Something clicked. For the first time all week, I wasn't forcing it. I'd found a window into the character—a strange window, but a window nonetheless.

I went in for the audition the following morning, confident that I'd made the character my own.

I got a callback, but I didn't book the role.

# COMING TO LOS ANGELES

## (TWICE)

The week after I graduated from college, I loaded up my only significant earthly possession—a blue 1994 Toyota Camry affectionately called the "Vomit Comet"—and drove to Los Angeles to begin my life as a film and television actor.

Before the trip, I took the car in for an inspection. The mechanic had strong opinions about the state of the vehicle. "Do not drive this car across the country," he said.

But, with no other car options available, I set off anyway.

I had everything planned out. The AC didn't work, so I rolled down the windows. Since the windows would be down, and the windshield had no UV protection, I'd get a nice bronzy tan in preparation for my new life in California. And the radio only worked maybe twenty percent of the time—that was actually going to be a problem.

I made the trip from Pittsburgh to LA in four days. Every night, I arrived at some out-of-the-way motel well after midnight, my body aching and stomach rumbling. And every single night, the motel clerk informed me that the only restaurant still open at that hour was Hooters. And every morning, I would wake up, brush my wings-stained teeth, and hit the road, praying that that night I would find someplace to eat that wasn't a Hooters.

But my prayers were never answered.

When I finally made it to Los Angeles, I made two promises to myself. One: I would never set foot in another Hooters. Two: I was done with cross-country road trips.

I broke both promises before the summer was out.

Shortly after I arrived in LA, my girlfriend at the time asked me to fly to Florida with her to pick up her car and drive it back to California. Being young, dumb, and extremely energetic, I agreed.

My girlfriend's car had all the amenities that mine had lacked. Actual working air-conditioning, a fully functional radio, tinted windows—and cup holders. We were living the high life.

But, embarking on my second cross-country road trip in as many months, I was again plagued by a series of pit stops in which Hooters was the only available food option. Eyes watering with regret, we gorged ourselves on plate after plate of Hooterstizers—the laziest portmanteau of all time—and prayed for anything, ideally a Denny's, to save us.

On the fourth day of the trip, just after we crossed the border between Arizona and California, I found something interesting on the map.

Just an hour out of the way was a place called the Salton Sea, and judging by the map, it was an oasis—a huge body of water in the middle of the desert. The idea of taking a break from the road, stretching our legs—maybe even jumping in the water—sounded pretty great.

We stopped at a gas station before heading down, bought some prepackaged sandwiches and sunscreen. Not quite speaking from experience yet, I bragged to my girlfriend, "You know, California has a lot of places like the Salton Sea. Little hidden gems. You're going to love it here."

There are a few things you notice as you approach the Salton Sea. The first is the smell. Maybe it was the scorching summer day—it was over a hundred degrees outside—but we could smell the Salton Sea miles before we arrived. I frantically tried to adjust the vents to stop letting in outside air, but it was too late. The stench of rotting fish was so bad you could taste it.

The second thing you notice is that you are the only people there. The few small towns around the eastern shore seem entirely devoid of life. Blocks of buildings are abandoned, relics of their former resort town glory. Once upon a time, when the lake was less salty, less polluted by the agriculture that surrounds it, the Salton Sea was actually a destination for the rich and famous—but no longer. Nowadays, not many people visit, especially in the middle of July.

We pulled into a state park with beach access to have a quick makeshift picnic. I think we got out of the car for about thirty seconds, just long enough to notice that the beach was blanketed with dead fish. Literally, dead fish as far as the eye could see. I'm not even sure we were walking on sand, or if it was just pulverized fish bones.

We ate our sandwiches in the car as we drove away.

I later learned that the Salton Sea is a major migratory pit stop for birds traveling along the Pacific flyway. Birds pass through, moving up and down the continent, and here I was traveling across it—our journeys intersecting at this strange, foul-smelling avian truck stop.

No, I take that back. It's not a truck stop: it's a Hooters. A Hooters for birds.

Sometimes when you're traveling across the United States, you stop there because it's the only place still open.

That afternoon, I arrived in Los Angeles for the second time in as many months. I made the same two promises to myself as before: no more cross-country road trips, no more Hooters.

This time I kept them.

# LUCY GOOSEY

A few months after I moved to Los Angeles, I woke up to a call from my agent, Steve. I'd been sleeping in a lot at the time, and I'd slept in again that day. I groggily picked up the phone, still half asleep, and tried to decipher what my agent was saying.

It took me a second to realize he was telling me to hurry up and get out of bed: I'd gotten a last-minute callback for a new ABC Family pilot called *Pretty Little Liars*.

I'd been meeting with casting directors regularly since I'd moved from Pittsburgh. I'd gone out for bit parts in TV, but this was my first pilot, and I had no idea what to expect. There's a difference between acting and auditioning, and I wasn't sure I was a strong auditioner. I could talk to casting directors all day about the quirks of classical theater training, but when it came to actually selling my version of a character to them, I was still very new to the game.

Despite my self-doubt, my representation kept pushing to get me in the room with casting directors all over town. They seemed to believe in my acting abilities, or at least in my bone structure. Their enthusiasm helped keep me motivated.

I'd been in to audition for this pilot once already—for the part of Ezra Fitz, a young high school English teacher. It'd gone decently well but hadn't been anything to write home about. Getting a callback came as a surprise. Steve gave me the breakdown for the *Pretty Little Liars* callback—he told me that I'd be reading across from Lucy Hale this time, the girl that had been cast as Ezra's underage love interest.

Before he got off the phone, Steve said, "Ian, not quite sure how to put this, but look nice, okay? Nice shirt, nice pants, wash your face. Don't mean to sound like your mom, but this one could be good for you."

Unfortunately, I didn't have much in the way of "nice" clothes. Student loans were hanging over my head like the sword of Damocles at the time, and buying new clothes seemed like a waste of money. I'd had to buy a suit earlier in the summer for a wedding, and had left all the tags on it so that I could return it after. About the only thing nice I owned was a blue button-down shirt. That morning it had pasta stains all over it from a raucous Italian dinner a few nights earlier, and I'd forgotten to do my laundry.

I rolled out of bed and surveyed my one-room apartment: all my possessions were strewn about within arm's length. Dangling on a suspicious-looking metal pipe sticking out of the ceiling was a hanger with my only other clothing option: a green V-neck sweater that I'd had since high school.

The sweater was from Hollister, and it had the company's seagull logo on the tag. I always liked that about it. It was like an inside joke between me and myself. Carrying that little bird everywhere with me always felt comforting, like a good luck charm.

Plus, it was also the only item of clothing I owned that didn't have holes in it. I wore it everywhere.

I threw myself in the shower, considered shaving but didn't have time, and tried to dry off as best I could. I didn't have AC, and on warm days the apartment would heat up like an oven. It was early October, and I should have been enjoying something hot and pumpkin-spiced, but it was sweltering outside.

There wasn't time to stand in front of the open refrigerator to cool off, which I did on a daily basis. I grabbed my trusty green sweater off the hangar and headed out to Warner Bros. studios in Burbank, where the audition was being held. Of course, my car didn't have AC either, and I could feel the beads of sweat on my back joining together to form small rivulets. It was as gross as it sounds.

Right before I walked into the casting office, I pulled the green sweater on and prayed that nobody would ask me about my clothing choices.

I walked into the office, which was thankfully cooled to an appropriate temperature for long sleeves.

Then I glanced around the room and started to sweat again.

The waiting area was filled with handsome model types. Guys who didn't own knives because they did all of their slicing and dicing with their razor-sharp jawlines. I recognized a few of them from their stints as sexy werewolves and morally loose ad men from the 1960s. Not only were these actors all phenomenally good-looking, they all had booked serious jobs before.

The only work I had under my belt at the time was a bit part in an indie film and a smoothie commercial I'd done in college.

"Ian Harding?"

A young woman with a clipboard approached and checked off my name.

"You'll be up in just a second."

I'd been to this office once before to meet with casting directors right after I moved to Los Angeles, and I knew there was a bathroom down the hall. I had to get away from everyone for just a second, make sure none of the cold pizza I'd had for breakfast on the drive over was stuck in my teeth.

In the bathroom I looked at myself in the mirror and doused my face with water, careful not to let any droplets get on my festive sweater. I started running through my lines in my head.

When I first started auditioning, I'd listened to music—usually fast-paced metal or hip-hop—to psych myself up. But I realized after a few auditions that I was going in and practically screaming my lines. So, I tweaked my routine to be a bit more meditative. It's been more effective so far than listening to Slipknot.

I closed my eyes, took a few slow and deliberate breaths, and, with my eyes closed, watched as my lines appeared in the dark space behind my eyelids.

The scene I was working on today involved me striking up a conversation with a woman at a bar in the middle of the afternoon. Cut to: we're making out in the women's restroom. It would end up being the scene that introduces my character in the first episode of the show.

The first time I read the pilot, I didn't quite know what to make of Ezra, but I felt like he and I somehow clicked. I felt a warmth about the role, a sort of natural rapport. I didn't want to go in and fuss with the part for this callback. I knew what I wanted to do with it.

From outside the bathroom I heard a door open and a female voice say something. Then a muffled chorus of heys and hellos from all the guys. I didn't want to keep casting waiting on me, so I ran a hand through my hair and gave myself a final once-over in the mirror.

Back in the lobby, the guys were all talking quietly. I sat down in an empty chair.

One of the sexy werewolves turned to me:

"You just missed her. Lucy Hale just walked by. The girl they cast as Aria."

Aria, the girl my character picks up at the bar. The entire room was buzzing about her.

"My friend did a short with her. He said she's single."

"Your friend's wrong, man. She's dating a guy from my cousin's acting class."

"Bullshit."

"I'm serious!"

"She's so hot."

A door opened at the far end of the room, and the casting assistant with the clipboard poked her head around the corner.

"Ian? We're ready for you."

The sexy werewolf called after me to break a leg as I walked across the room.

The shades were all pulled down on the windows in the audition room, and it took a second for my eyes to adjust. The only source of light was a bright lamp mounted on a C-stand. There were half a dozen people seated behind a camera on one side of the room.

"Hey man, good to see you again," a guy called out from behind the camera.

"Yeah you too, bud," I replied, realizing that "bud" might have sounded a little too chummy.

There were familiar faces in the room, but new ones too. The woman to my left—I was pretty sure she was the writer of the show. Or the creator? Both?

The guy to her right—Bob, was it? He had seemed like a nice guy the last time I read for the part. I figured I would try and keep him laughing, maybe crack a joke about all the look-alikes waiting outside.

Gayle, the casting director, whom I'd met a few days prior, gave me a big smile. "Good to see you again, Ian," she said. "Have a seat there and go ahead and slate whenever you're ready."

I sat down, a hand over my eyes to shade the glare of the light over the camera.

"Hi," a voice chirped to my side.

I totally hadn't seen her: right next to me, smiling expectantly, was Lucy Hale.

"Oh hey," I said. "Didn't see you there."

"Hot out, isn't it?" she teased, eyeing my sweater.

"I just like Christmas a lot," came out of my mouth. That didn't entirely make sense.

She grinned mischievously at me.

There was something about her that I recognized immediately, or recognized in her. We'd never met before, but there was something familiar, something comforting about Lucy. Perhaps the way she looked at me in that moment felt open, receptive. Like she was taking me in as opposed to merely appraising me.

It wasn't cinematic: sparks didn't fly, orchestral music didn't well up as we gazed into each other's eyes. It was a simpler moment. Quieter. Two people stuck in a whirlwind of expectation and excitement—we each somehow understood who the other was.

"I'm Ian, by the way," I said, leaning forward to shake her hand.

"Lucy," she said, a slight smile spreading across her face.

"Whenever you're ready," Gayle said.

I sat, took a deep breath, and we began.

Lucy's line went something like, "Oh, I love this song."

I nodded. There wasn't any music playing, but I nodded. I looked into Lucy's eyes, and it suddenly dawned on me what the scene was about. It wasn't a love scene at all. I didn't need to kiss her, or have sex with her, or make her my wife.

I wanted to understand her. It was that simple. I wanted to know everything I possibly could about this woman.

Somebody coughed. I had a line to say.

"B-twenty-six!" I blurted out. It was the number of the song on the jukebox at the bar we were supposed to be sitting in.

Lucy's eyes went wide in surprise. She hadn't expected the line to come out like that—neither had I.

We were both surprised, and because we were both surprised, the moment was suddenly alive. Fresh. We were listening to each other, actually communicating. There was chemistry.

We read through the scene again, the second time the

dialogue rolled out crisper than the first. I wanted to read through the scene once more. I was having too much fun.

But all too soon my time was up.

I looked around at the faces in the room. At the end of every audition, there's a moment, usually no longer than the time it takes to look up from your script, when, for a fraction of a second, you see the next few years of your life align. When you start out as an actor, this is the moment you live for.

Marlene—that was her name!—the creator of the show, thanked me for coming in as she scribbled on the pages on her lap.

"Yup, good job," Gayle said. I think she was smiling.

Headshots were shuffled. Pens scratched paper.

"Thank you!" I threw out to no one in particular.

I grabbed my keys and phone, which I had apparently set down on the floor at some point.

I turned back to Lucy.

"Thank you for everything," I said.

"Oh! You too. Don't die from heat exhaustion in that sweater," she said.

I walked back out through the waiting room, waved to the werewolf and told him something like "go get 'em," and headed for the parking lot. I waited until I got all the way outside before ripping off my sweat-drenched sweater.

On the way home, my phone buzzed. Vikram, my manager, was calling. I pulled over to take the call.

"How'd it go?" he asked.

"I really have no idea."

"That can be good."

"Yeah."

I sat for a moment, mulling over the audition.

"This one was different," I said.

Vikram waited for me to continue.

I put the phone on speaker and laid it on the dashboard, freeing my hands to gesture what my mouth couldn't articulate.

"Lucy Hale was in the room. It was a chemistry read, right? I was surprised at how easy it was. It was like hanging out with an old friend. It was weird."

"Ian, all of that sounds like a good thing."

"Maybe you're right," I conceded.

"No, I am right, because they want you to go in for a network test."

"You already knew!?" I yelled at the phone.

Vikram chuckled. "I wanted to know your thoughts first!"

Several more rounds of callbacks followed. And every round there were fewer and fewer of us in the waiting room. Lucy and I read together in front of different people in different rooms, and we got to hang out a little bit, too. We were becoming fast friends.

Finally, there were just two of us left trying out for the role of Ezra. Me and one other guy. He was Canadian. The pilot, and possibly the entire show, was going to be shot in Vancouver, so my agents had warned me that he was the financially responsible option for the studio.

On the day of the final producer session, I arrived early. I was sitting in my car in the parking lot, going over my lines with my eyes closed, when I heard a tap on the window. It was Lucy. She grinned and waved. I rolled down my window.

"Schmian!" she yelled. Lucy loves nicknames.

"Hey, Lucy Goosey."

"How you feeling?" she asked. "Excited?"

"Nervous," I said. "I'm feeling really, really nervous."

"I know what you mean. Between you and me, I hope you get it. It'd be really fun to work together."

We went inside, shook hands with the producers, and I auditioned my heart out one last time.

I was going to miss this. With all of the other actors I'd met in Los Angeles, acting had felt like work. I showed up and I did my job. With Lucy, it felt like two kids in a sandbox. We were constantly surprising one another.

After the audition, I felt a strange hollowness. It was my last audition for the show. There was nothing else I could do now. And I wasn't ready for this all to end.

I wanted this role.

Back in my neighborhood, I was circling the block looking for a parking space, when my phone started to buzz again. It was Steve, my agent. I put the phone on speaker.

"Hey!" I said.

The voice on the phone was somber.

"Ian, hey," he said. "This a good time?"

"What's up?" I said.

"I've got bad news . . ."

I stopped the car in the middle of the street. It was over. It had been a nice fantasy, but I should have known better than to get my hopes up.

"Let's hear it."

"Yeah. It's just—do you have any warm clothes?"

In the passenger seat next to me was the green sweater that I'd worn to that first callback. One of these days I was going to remember to get it washed.

"Yeah, I've got a sweater or two," I said. "Why?"

"I hear that Canada is cold in November."

". . ."

"So you'll need to pack some warm clothes since you're going to be up there shooting for a month. You got the role, Ian. Knocked it out of the park. Congrats!"

". . ."

"Ian, are you there?"

"Goddamnit, Steve!" I shouted. "My emotions are not a pipe for you to play upon!"

Steve chuckled and took my outburst for what it truly was: tremendous excitement.

After we got off the phone, I looked back over at the sweater with the seagull on its tag.

When I got my first paycheck, I went and got it dry-cleaned.

## IL BUIO OLTRE
## LA SIEPE

Every once in a while I'll get a text from a friend asking me to help identify a bird they've seen. Sometimes it's a blurry photo. Sometimes it's a description of what the bird looked like. It makes me feel like an ornithological Google.

Keegan Allen, who plays Toby Cavanaugh on *Pretty Little Liars*, frequently texts me pictures to figure out what he's looking at.

Keegs is an amazing photographer. He's even published a coffee table book of his photographs—so it's always fun when he sends me an out-of-focus picture of a tree or fuzzy telephone wires. Sometimes he'll send me a photo of the sky with a tiny black dot way in the distance and ask me what it is.

I know Keegan's making fun of me. He once texted me a

voice recording of himself cawing. I told him it sounded like a young Woody Harrelson crying in the shower. He texted back to say that I was "extremely bad at bird IDs," then two minutes later texted again to say that birds were stupid and he hoped he hadn't hurt my "widdle birdy feewings."

To his credit, he does send me photos and recordings of real birds, too. He once sent me a recording of a nighthawk that he took while he was visiting his mom up in Northern California. I'm not always able to identify the birds when people ask, but I definitely knew what that one was. His mom now texts me any time she has a question about birds, too.

The most common question I get from people in Los Angeles is: "There's a bird outside my window that sings all night long. What the hell is it, and how do I make it stop?"

It's a northern mockingbird, and they're the worst. If they were human, they'd be telemarketers: always calling at the worst possible time. And, for the record, I don't know how to make them go away.

It's the single males that stay up late—bachelor mockingbirds will sing all night long. Like frat boys, they spend all their time after the sun goes down loudly advertising that they want to have sex. Once they settle into a relationship, they start sleeping again and just sing during the day.

There was one that lived in the bushes outside my bedroom window in my old house in Laurel Canyon. Every night, like clockwork, it'd start singing at one in the morning.

Mockingbirds are known for their ability to mimic other sounds. When they sing, they'll cycle through a bunch of different songs. Besides just other birdcalls, they'll meow like cats and bark like dogs. In cities, they'll loudly imitate car alarms—which is charming.

These birds are easy to hate, but people aren't the only ones who hate mockingbirds. They also hate themselves.

Mockingbirds are fiercely, fiercely territorial. They'll dive-bomb other mockingbirds, shriek at them, flash their wings menacingly—anything to get the other bird to go away.

The problem is, the other mockingbirds they're attacking often aren't birds at all—they're mirrors. Male mockingbirds will attack their own reflections for hours at a time, just bashing their heads against the glass. If you asked a mockingbird to list its greatest enemies, it would probably tell you cats, hawks, owls, and that-son-of-a-bitch-in-the-bay-window-oh-my-God-I-want-to-kill-him-so-bad.

One of my neighbors down the street has to keep plastic grocery bags wrapped around her car's side-view mirrors. If she doesn't, a mockingbird will sit on the side of her car all day, pooping on her windows and periodically swooping down to smash itself into the mirrors until they crack.

They're crazy.

But I get it. I mean, I don't wake up every morning and head-butt my bathroom mirror before I go downstairs to make coffee, but I get where they're coming from. I really don't like watching myself on-screen, either.

Have you ever recorded your own voice and played it back? You probably thought something like, *That's not what I sound like ... right? That's not actually my voice.* Our voices don't actually sound the way they do in our heads.

Watching yourself act on-screen is the same, except it's not just your voice anymore: you've got to deal with how you look, how you move, how you react. There's that same strange disconnect between what you think you look like and how it all appears on TV.

I've never been able to really enjoy watching myself. It's a little bit eerie and a little bit unnerving. I'll think I portrayed a certain character one way in front of the camera, but then, watching it later on TV, I'll zero in on specific physical quirks or intonations that I wasn't aware of. Body language I wasn't conscious of using.

Still, even if deep down it feels unnatural, I know that watching my own footage is an excellent tool for me as an actor. Sports players watch tapes of themselves swinging bats and throwing footballs to figure out how to improve their form, and actors regularly do the same thing.

When I watch myself, the goal is to put some distance between me and the version of me that's on-screen. I want to judge my performance objectively, so that I can develop as an actor. If I notice that I always react a certain way to a certain type of line, I can take that information and begin to change that habit into a conscious choice. Doing so can give me greater range and control over how I come across. It broadens my acting.

When I first started out on *Pretty Little Liars*, it was even more difficult than usual for me to watch myself. I'd watch new episodes but would find myself squirming when I came on-screen. Occasionally, I got so uncomfortable that I'd have to turn off the TV. Eventually, I stopped watching altogether.

But I really wanted to get better, and I recently happened upon a solution: Italian dubbing.

Turns out, I have absolutely no problem watching myself on-screen as long as I am watching the dubbed version of my show that airs in Italy. The guy whose voice they use for mine is named Francesco Venditti, and his voice is—well, it's just goddamn poetry to listen to. I don't understand Italian, but it's so much nicer than listening to my own voice.

We've never met, but Francesco has helped me get over the discomfort I used to feel watching myself on-screen. He's been like a plastic bag over the side-view mirror for me. Finally, I can relax and enjoy the show.

# DEATH AND

# LOONS

A lot of people get killed on *Pretty Little Liars*—it's just that kind of show.

Funeral scenes are some of my favorite to shoot. There are one or two each season, and they usually involve most of the regular cast. The scenes when we're all working together are sort of like cast reunions. The mood on set is even more lighthearted than usual.

A lot of the funeral scenes are filmed in a little white chapel on the Warner Bros. back lot in Burbank. It's not an actual chapel: it's only ever used for filming. You can see the same exterior and interior of the building in just about every season. It pops up at the end of season one, for example, when Spencer's brother-in-law Ian Thomas tries to push her off the bell tower.

We actually film almost all of the show on the Warner Bros. lot, and there are a handful of houses and buildings that provide nearly all of the exterior shots. You may recognize some of the same buildings on *Gilmore Girls* or *Heart of Dixie*—they're regularly repurposed for different projects.

There's a courthouse and a fire department, which are two sides of the same building. There are wooded areas for when the girls have to run for their lives through a forest. Some of the trees are real, some are made of plastic.

There's an art museum—or at least the façade of one—where I take Aria on our first real date on the show in season one . . . in a limousine.

Yes, a limo. On a high school teacher's salary.

A few seasons back, the building that was Toby's house got real-life termites. It had to be torn down, so the writers came up with the idea to have "A"—the show's unremitting and anonymous villain—blow it up. I was there for the explosion—and, for the record, it was awesome.

The only thing we don't have on the lot, which you'd think would be useful for a show like ours, is a good cemetery. I'm sure there are plenty of reasons why Warner Bros. doesn't have a cemetery on the lot, but with so many people dying on *PLL*, once in a blue moon we have to leave set to film in a real one.

When you see tombstones on the show, they're usually real.

In season one, for instance, we filmed Ian Thomas's burial at Mountain View Cemetery in Altadena, about an hour east of the Warner Bros. lot.

I understand that sometimes you have to travel to get the right shot, and that sometimes certain locations are off-limits or prohibitively expensive to shoot at. It's still a bit funny to me, though, that we drove an hour off the lot to shoot in a cemetery—because there's another one directly across the street from Warner Bros.

Forest Lawn–Hollywood Hills is a beautiful sight. The cemetery is made up of rolling green hills dotted with towering pine trees, and lush green lawns are manicured to a golf course level of precision.

Once, a few years back, I went to see Torrey DeVitto, who plays Melissa on the show, play violin with the Burbank Philharmonic at a performance space there. Before the concert, I took a stroll through the tombstones. Looking up, I saw a small flock of white-throated swifts far overhead, riding the wind gusting over the mountains of Griffith Park, which the cemetery backs up to.

Dying is big business in Southern California, and I've seen Forest Lawn advertisements at Dodger Stadium during baseball games, and there's even a Forest Lawn kiosk at the Glendale Galleria mall—it's right above the food court.

There are six Forest Lawn cemeteries in Los Angeles. I drive by two of them just on my way to work. There's Forest Lawn–Hollywood Hills, of course, the one directly across the street from Warner Bros., and then there's Forest Lawn–Memorial Park, which is nestled on a quiet hilltop at the southern edge of Glendale.

I've been over to Forest Lawn–Memorial Park a few times. Long, winding roads cut through the graveyard, making their way slowly up the hill. The higher you drive, the more expansive the views of the city become. At the top, there's a gorgeous panoramic vista: Glendale to the east, with Pasadena beyond it; the Los Angeles River to the west; the City of Burbank to the north; and the skyscrapers of downtown just on the horizon to the south.

There's a massive auditorium up at the top, with a 195-foot-long painting of the crucifixion. Next door, in the auditorium's shadow, is a museum. The front half has rotating exhibits, usually contemporary work with a focus on Hollywood. The back half is where they keep the permanent collection—a seemingly disconnected array of artifacts and treasures. You half expect to find a piece of the One True Cross stashed away between the gold chainmail and the paintings of duchess's dogs. It's like a conquistador's messy garage.

I really like spending time at Forest Lawn. Cemeteries can be peaceful, even pleasant, and I don't mean that in a creepy, Edgar Allan Poe–ish way. I don't go over to Forest Lawn to pay my respects, or commune with the dead, or anything like that. There aren't specific gravestones I visit, though it's always fun to see all the weird last names people have. I also don't go to visit the celebrities buried there, of which there are many—Elizabeth Taylor, Clark Gable, Michael Jackson.

I go because there's great birding in cemeteries.

Seriously. In big cities, cemeteries are often some of the best places to find birds. Cemeteries are acres of land unobstructed by buildings or other major human development. They're a lot like parks: well-maintained trees, shrubbery, and expansive grass lawns—perfect for birds.

I don't think I would have ever thought to try birding in a cemetery if I hadn't read about it online. The first time I went to a cemetery to look at birds, it was because of a rare-bird alert. A group of birders had seen a scissor-tailed flycatcher in a cemetery in Santa Monica, and they posted about it on an online forum.

Birding is a solitary hobby. You spend most of your time alone in nature, looking and listening intently to the world around you. There are some birding groups, but for the most part birders keep to themselves.

That all changes when there's a rare-bird alert—they're the ice cream socials of the birding world. Birders come out in droves to see rare birds when they've strayed far from their normal range. Everybody drops what they're doing and hops in their cars and races over to the spot of the last sighting.

I subscribe to a forum that people post on whenever they see rare or unusual birds in Los Angeles. I only learned about it a couple of years ago, and since then, I've been spending way too much time checking for updates. Maybe once or twice a day, somebody will see something unusual and report in. Sometimes it will be a rare-bird alert, sometimes it will be a woman in Hollywood asking for advice on how to get a snowy egret to stop eating the house finches in her yard. Either way, the online forums are an incredible tool.

Birders move in flocks when they get together. A rare-bird alert will go out, saying that an unusual bird has been spotted that morning at such-and-such location. A good alert will be followed by a flurry of confirmations from individuals. Then everybody loads their gear into their cars and drives, all the while dangerously checking their phones for updates, to the site of the last spotting. Once they arrive, the birders gather into a tight huddle, craning their necks this way and that to see if anyone can spot anything. For a while, nothing will happen.

Then, after ten or fifteen minutes, a lone scout on the other side of the park will shout that they've spotted the lazuli bunting or whatever bird it is that day, and the group will clatter together loudly across the park in pursuit. Thirty or forty birders zigzagging about in a binoculared pack. This mass of bodies will inevitably scare the bird away, so by the time the group arrives by the scout's side, the bird will have moved on.

A few years back, I think it was in May, an alert went out that an arctic loon had become stranded in a small town just east of Los Angeles. I expected it to stick around for only a few days, but it was still there in July, and I decided to go find it.

To be clear, arctic loons have no business being in Southern California. It's exciting news when they fly as far south as British Columbia. They have evolved to survive in extremely cold climates—their genetic makeup designed to flourish in the icy tundra of western Siberia, not the rowdy strip malls of West Covina.

The arctic loon had been spotted in a place called Puddingstone Lake. I drove out there one day to try and see it.

Walking around, I passed more barbecues than you'd see in a whole summer of Fourth of Julys. Super-cool lifeguards sat perched at intervals all along the shore.

I pulled out my binoculars to see if the loon might be out on the water. I surveyed the lake. All I could see were mallards and people swimming. Babies bobbed up and down, overinflated floaties manacled to their pudgy little arms. A middle-school boy was trying to convince his girlfriend there were eels in the water. It was exactly what you would expect from a place called Puddingstone Lake: just the cutest stuff imaginable.

I put the binoculars away and decided to walk along the shore to see if I could catch a glimpse of the loon a little farther down.

About half a mile on, I passed a swimming hole where eight or ten kids were splashing around. It was significantly less crowded than the beach I had just left. There was a bored-looking lifeguard sitting up high on his stand.

I wasn't having any luck spotting this arctic loon, and even though I didn't expect anyone else to care about it, I tried my luck and asked him if he'd seen any strange-looking birds out on the water that morning.

"You mean the arctic loon?" he said, his eyes invisible behind his mirrored aviators.

"I, uh, yeah. You know about that?" I stammered.

"Of course, dude. Loon's been here for like a month. It's a pretty chill little bird."

"Do you know where it might be today?"

"I think he's over by Sailboat Cove right now."

"That's not a real place," I said.

He shrugged. "I didn't name it."

Sure enough, about a hundred yards off from a dock with sail-boats near it, which I assumed was Sailboat Cove, I saw it: the arctic loon, sitting out on the water.

It looked really lost.

It disappeared underwater briefly, popping back up a few yards away from where it had been swimming. I imagined it was trying to stay as cool as possible given how hot it was out-side.

I associate loons so strongly with their call, and just watch-ing the bird, I began to imagine its plaintive wail.

Every summer, my family goes up to New England for a couple of weeks. There's a lake we go to, and visiting it is almost a religious experience for me. The lake is filled with loons—hundreds of them. If you stand on the shore at dusk and listen, the place sounds haunted.

My aunt Jules loves loons. When the family arrives at the lake, before we even unpack the car, she will walk solemnly to the shore and stand completely still, staring out at the loons on the water. She'll stand like that for about ten minutes, then will give the lake a slight nod and return to the car to carry in the rest of the luggage. Other than Saint Peter's Basilica, I've never seen anything else give my aunt pause like that. She is a ball of energy—frantic, kind, and opinionated. But the loons silence her.

As I stood there now, not at the lake from my childhood but on a shore in San Dimas, staring at a totally different species of loon from the ones I'd grown up with, something occurred to me.

Many rare bird sightings only happen when something has gone wrong. Whether blown off course or just extremely lost, somehow an individual bird becomes separated from its flock and finds itself thousands of miles away from home. The land is unfamiliar, the climate sometimes deadly.

When an arctic loon gets lost in a lake in Southern California, it's hard to imagine it's ever going to make it back home to the icy north. And if it doesn't, it's likely going to die. So, in a case like this, the rare bird alert that went out for the loon was also, in a sense, its obituary. It's sad—seeing this magnificent bird and knowing that it probably only has a short while left to live.

There was a voice in my head that told me to respond to this tragedy the way we respond to so many others: to take a picture with my phone and drive home.

But something felt wrong about that approach. Maybe it was that tourism didn't feel like an appropriate response to death. Whatever it was, I didn't feel comfortable standing there and watching a lost animal float helplessly on the waves of a lake that would soon envelop it.

I wanted to swim out and grab the loon, stash it in a suitcase, and fly it up north, as far north as we could go before my fingers froze solid. Then I would fling open my suitcase and shout, "You're free, loon! Free to spend your days swimming in the icy waters of the north!"

But conservation doesn't work like that. In the movies, when you go with your gut, everything turns out okay. You can just go and save the day because it's obvious to everyone around you that what you're doing is inherently the right thing to do.

In the real world there's paperwork, borders, agricultural restrictions, holding periods, smuggling laws. There are ecological standards and conservation rules that change from nation to nation. Ornithologists—and even lifeguards—knew that the bird was there on Puddingstone Lake, and there was nothing anyone could do about it. Sometimes, the best thing to do with nature is to leave it alone.

Driving away from the lake, I kept thinking about it.

As I got on to the highway, I passed another Forest Lawn cemetery—turns out they have one in Covina, right next to the lake.

It occurred to me, as I looked out my window, that the last

few times I'd been to a cemetery, it'd been for a concert or to film the show or to wander around and look at birds. I'd been to a graveyard a couple of times that year, and it'd always been fun.

Getting to see the loon had felt like a funeral.

# SPRING

# MIGRATION

One of the great things about birding is that you can do it anywhere in the world.

In Paris for a fan convention? Head over to the Cimetière du Père-Lachaise, visit the graves of Oscar Wilde and Jim Morrison, and see what birds you can find in the trees overhead. Or maybe you're in New York City for a press junket. Easy. Take an afternoon and go try to find Pale Male, a famous red-tailed hawk that lives on the Upper East Side, named for his pale face.

You can tack birding on to any normal trip with the simple addition of binoculars.

Or, you can go all out. Once, on a trip to Seattle with Sophia for a wedding, I hired a birding guide for a morning.

We were out in a marsh, and the guide played a recording of a Virginia rail on a handheld speaker. A little shadow picked its way through a thicket of reeds, was in view for about five seconds or so, and then silently vanished back into the dense stalks. Spotting a Virginia rail hadn't been the point of the trip— they're usually next to impossible to see—but, like I said before, birds are everywhere.

I'd gotten back into birding a few years earlier on the trip to Big Bear, but as of the sixth season of the show, I'd never been on a trip outside of Los Angeles specifically to see birds. I was daunted by the idea.

Sure, I'd look at birds while out walking the dogs. Or I'd go on hikes with friends and wander off when I saw something interesting. On weekends, I'd drive out to the Ballona Wetlands, just north of LAX in Marina del Rey, to see what I could find. There's a path along a swamp there, and you can usually see ducks and herons. In the near distance, double-decker Airbuses take off, on their way to distant shores.

I'd been treating birding as an excuse to get away from work. It was a reason to get outside, not a reason to get on one of those planes.

Last year I decided to go someplace new with the sole purpose of birding my face off. This was big for me. It was springtime: time for new growth, new life. Birds were in the air.

Seriously, birds were in the air. A lot of them. Every spring, millions of birds migrate up from Central and South America to their summer breeding grounds in North America. There are a couple of prime spots to see them, natural bottlenecks on the migration paths, where the chances of seeing normally hard-to-find species are pretty good.

So I pulled the trigger: I booked a flight to Houston.

About an hour and a half east of the city, there's a small bump in the land on the coast—just a little rise, caused by a salt dome that got squeezed up from below the earth's surface. It's a geological pimple. High Island, as it's called, is the highest natural coastal feature from the Yucatán to Alabama. It's a whopping thirty-eight feet above sea level.

That may not sound special, but it is. Imagine you've been stranded at sea for a few days, and you finally spot land on the horizon. Even if that land was Trenton, New Jersey, you'd be excited.

That's what High Island is like for birds. Because it's slightly higher than the surrounding coastal prairie, it's the first speck of mainland that a lot of birds see as they make their way over six hundred miles across the Gulf of Mexico. And once they reach High Island, there's plentiful water and food and trees to rest in. Migrating birds stop here by the thousands in the spring to rest and refuel before continuing their journey northward.

On rare occasions, a strong storm out of the north will coincide with a wave of neotropical migrants flying up over the Gulf. When this happens, birds will come in to land at High Island en masse. It's called a "fallout." Every limb of every tree—and even the ground—is littered with tired birds: warblers, vireos, orioles, tanagers, buntings. All the stunning small birds that pass through ever year but you never see.

And you can't see these birds in such concentrated numbers anywhere else, ever.

All of this is why High Island is a Mecca for bird lovers. Why it's talked about with a kind of hushed reverence—the way your drunk uncle talks about Woodstock. You had to have been there, man.

I booked the trip to Houston for mid-April. We had just started shooting season seven of *Pretty Little Liars*. I only ever know my shooting schedule a few days in advance, but I figured I could change the flight last-minute if there was a conflict.

I tried to cozy up to the producers, hoping they would let me know what my schedule was for the rest of the month. But they didn't know the schedule, either.

The whole process of making the show comes down to the wire every week. I usually don't learn my lines until the day before we shoot. It's not that I don't want to: I can't. Script rewrites happen up until the very last minute, and the head writer on each episode is always on set in case any last-minute rewrites or script changes are necessary. There's an elegant chaos to it all.

I was getting increasingly giddy about the trip, and anxious to get going. It was distracting me from my work. During breaks from shooting, I'd even started studying bird flashcards.

Tyler Blackburn—who plays Caleb Rivers on the show— came up to me one day while I was running through the cards and asked what I was doing. I told him about the trip. He asked when I was going, and I told him the second-to-last week in April, right at the height of the migration.

"So, you're going to High Island for four-twenty?" he asked.

"Yeah, why?"

Tyler grinned mischievously.

"High Island . . . four-twenty . . ."

"It's not like that, man. It's for the birds!"

Not surprisingly, there were last-minute schedule changes, so I had to push the trip back a week. And then I had to push it back again.

My personal and work lives were at an impasse. It looked less and less likely that I would even get to go.

By the time I actually got on the plane at LAX, it was the second week of May. It was cutting it close—the migration was winding down—but I had to go.

In the seat to the left of me was my buddy John. He was in the class below mine at Carnegie, and we've been friends for years. When he was a freshman, he used my home address for his fake ID. To my right was Walter, the guy I'd seen the hooded merganser with at Big Bear. I'd convinced them to tag along. They're both writers, so they can work from just about anywhere.

Sitting on the plane, I was excited. I couldn't contain myself. The small child sitting in the row in front of me kept turning around to glare at my bouncing knee, which was shaking his chair. We hadn't even taken off yet, and I was already vibrating with glee.

"It's okay, dude. I don't like to fly either," Walter said to me, his face a little pale.

"You seem pretty calm," I said.

"Oh, good," he replied. "I'm not." He closed his eyes like he was going to take a nap.

John was straddling an overstuffed backpack. He kept rooting around in it and pulling out snack-sized packages of peanut M&M's.

"John, did you bring anything besides candy?"

"Of course I did," he said.

"What do you have that's not candy?" Walter asked, his eyes still shut.

"Let's find out," John said, reaching into his backpack. He pulled out a king-sized package of Skittles, a gallon freezer bag filled with candy corn, and a tray of Oreos. Finally, he held up a can of Pringles. "See? I've got chips, too."

John is fit, yet has the diet of a hummingbird. He consumes more sugar than should be legal yet still manages to look like a college soccer player.

Walter also looks collegiately athletic, though this is achieved through what he calls "old Russian man workouts"—twenty minutes on the stationary bike, forty in the sauna—and surfing.

This was also not Walter's first trip to High Island, so he knew what we were in for.

As we pushed back from the jet bridge, Walter leaned forward and looked out the window.

"High Island is one of my favorite places on earth," he said. "If we get lucky, the trees will be filled with birds—like Christmas ornaments."

He leaned back into his seat and closed his eyes again. I couldn't wait to see it myself.

I pulled out a magazine I'd picked up at the terminal. It had caught my eye as I passed a newsstand. I don't normally buy *Cosmopolitan*, but this one had my costar Shay Mitchell on the cover—and there was an article about a beach body diet that said I could eat all the pizza I wanted, so I had to learn more about that.

John leaned over, looking at my reading material. "And you're giving me shit for bringing candy?"

It was dark when we got into Houston. Just past 9:00 P.M. We waited for our bags at baggage claim—something syrupy was leaking out of John's suitcase onto the carousel. He grabbed the bag, and told us to ignore it. We didn't press the issue.

Bags collected, we rode the rent-a-car shuttle to the offsite lot. When I'd made a reservation for the car, I'd looked online to find a good price, and a certain vehicle had caught my eye. I hadn't told the guys about it yet—they were in for a surprise.

We all gathered around the vehicle in the lot. It glowed a ghostly white in the darkness.

The minivan's siren song was impossible to resist—for some. Walter was thrilled by the choice of vehicle. John, however, had serious concerns that we would look like a gang of bird-loving pedophiles. That didn't bother me. If you put the two parts of my life together, that's what I am.

Walter and I rock-paper-scissored to see who'd be driving— John claimed the entire back row for himself—and then I drove us away from the airport toward the hustle and bustle of the Houston suburbs.

We stopped on our way into town for bratwurst at a late-night beer garden just east of downtown. It was a shack in the middle of an otherwise vacant lot, with wooden picnic tables and strands of lights strewn between the trees.

Walter was back by the car. I glanced over to see him shielding his eyes, staring up into the inky darkness.

Dipping and looping overhead was a common nighthawk.

Its long, thin wings flapped erratically. It called: a two-tone electronic chirp. Then it vanished into the dark.

"I used to see those after our high school football games," John said, following my gaze. "They'd fly around the stadium lights."

"I didn't know you played football," I said.

"I was the mascot," he said proudly.

"They fired him after one game," Walter said, as he walked back over to join us.

Later, sitting at a picnic table, John put down his bratwurst and shook his head. "This is unbelievable. This modern world, you know? I can wake up in Los Angeles, go to work, meet my girlfriend for lunch, go home to discover that my dog's eaten a condom, and still have time to travel across the country for bratwurst. All in one day. The magic of air travel, man."

Walter and I stared at him.

"John, did your dog eat a—"

"You're missing the point," he interrupted. "The point is that we *flew* here. Just like those birds."

He gestured upward. There weren't any birds. The nighthawk was long gone. "All in one day, you know?"

The next morning, we woke up at 5:00 A.M. We wanted to get out to High Island close to sunrise, to see if we could catch any stragglers that had stayed overnight. And new birds often come in early.

We tried to make coffee at the hotel, but the machine was intimidatingly complex—figuring out which button was "on" was like solving the riddle of the Sphinx.

We stopped at a Starbucks for caffeine, then headed east out of town on I-10. It was the same highway I'd taken in the opposite direction on that cross-country drive from Florida to LA.

The week before, thunderstorm after thunderstorm had wreaked havoc across the region. Houston had flooded. Like take-a-canoe-to-work flooded—and there were still sandbags scattered along the sides of the highway. This rain was exactly what we wanted—thunderstorms equal good birds.

Eventually we turned off the I-10 and started heading south to the coast. The land was flat and swampy. There was agriculture and farmland. Oil pumps were scattered in loose clusters like oversized grasshoppers. We crossed over a bridge that rose high enough to allow tanker ships to pass by in the channel below, and then drove up into the small town of High Island.

By that point, the caffeine had hit. We were raring to go. We pulled up in front of a preserve called the Boy Scout Woods and jumped out of the minivan like a SWAT team. We speed-walked over to the entrance, then speed-walked back to the car when we realized how dense the cloud of mosquitoes following us was. We sprayed ourselves down with bug repellent the way teenage boys use Axe body spray and headed back to the entrance.

Across the street there were a few residential houses. Some of them trailer homes. Directly next to the preserve were more. We were, in fact, just a hundred yards or so from the main road through town.

We walked into the Boy Scout Woods through a gate in a chain-link fence, probably meant to keep out cats. House cats kill more than a billion birds a year in the United States. A billion—that's not a typo.

It was basically an overgrown neighborhood park. One wrong turn and we'd end up in somebody's backyard.

Just past the entrance, a set of wooden grandstands faced a small clearing. At the end of the clearing, a hose hung out of a tree, dripping water for birds to drink and bathe in. I'd seen pictures online of the grandstand filled with birders, all aiming their spotting scopes and binoculars at the drip.

But now, the grandstands were empty. There were only a few people poking around the woods, and nobody was seeing much.

It was still early. It was a Monday. I assumed the birds would pick up as the sun rose a little higher. Or maybe birds just hate Mondays.

Two hours went by and it was still slow. Walter seemed bummed by the low bird turnout, but I was excited. We saw a few different species of warbler: magnolia, black-throated green, and black-and-white. All new for me.

We hopped back into the car and drove over to the Smith Oaks, another preserve about a mile away.

There's a large rookery there, and we happened upon a Japanese tour group all silently taking photos of the nesting egrets and roseate spoonbills. They were all glued to cameras on tripods with monstrous telephoto lenses.

I walked over to see what they were looking at, and the tree next to me moved. I had totally missed a guy decked out head to toe in camouflage standing on a limb right next to my head, and I nearly shit myself when he shifted position.

Farther down the path, we got a good view of a pair of snowy egrets. John perked up. He put his hands around his mouth and did a perfect imitation of their call. The birds looked around, trying to figure out where the sound had come from. I turned to him:

"What the hell was that?" I asked.

"I was an egret for Animal Projects," he said.

"Seriously?"

"Yeah, man. What were you?"

"I was a jellyfish."

"That makes sense."

We walked through the woods near the rookery for another hour or so. I spotted a yellow-billed cuckoo—another new bird—slipping its way through the foliage at the top of a huge live oak tree, but it flew off before Walter or John could see it. Otherwise, it was very quiet. There might have been more birders than actual birds that day. And there weren't many birders.

We stuck around for a few more hours anyway. We kept hoping a new wave of birds might arrive—but it never came. Eventually, we decided to call it quits and took the ferry to Galveston for a late lunch. On the way, we stopped to look at shorebirds on the beach, where I picked up a few more new species: black-bellied whistling duck, gull-billed tern, and magnificent frigatebird.

That night, John dragged us to a Dave & Buster's. As we were standing around an air hockey table, drinking beer and scratching the mosquito bites on our arms, we discussed options for the next day. Walter and I were both in agreement that High Island would probably be a bust again. It turns out, it probably would have been a great place to visit on 4/20. Just not in mid-May. The birds, for the most part, were already farther north.

John took his eye off the puck—

"Guys! I have an idea," he said. "Let's go to the Space Center tomorrow!"

Walter scored on him. He turned to me. "What about trying to find the red-cockaded woodpecker?"

"They have those around here?" I asked.

John cut in: "They also have Space Centers around here!"

"They're endangered," Walter said. "But there's a place not too far away where we can see them," he said.

"Sold," I said. "Let's do it."

Our destination the next morning was the W. G. Jones State Forest—one of the last places in Texas where you can still see the red-cockaded woodpecker. It was directly north of us, about an hour away.

We were on the road just as the sun was coming up.

At one point on the drive, I looked into the rearview mirror and saw John drinking a Red Bull. This was after we'd already stopped for coffee. I asked for a sip and took the can away from him. He was hyper enough already. He pulled another can out of his backpack and popped the tab.

He stared at me in the mirror, not breaking eye contact: "Don't toy with me, Ian," he said.

We were prepared to spend the morning deep in the woods, but W. G. Jones caught us by surprise. It really didn't seem all that remote: like High Island, the forest was bordered by urban sprawl.

We turned off the highway into a dirt parking lot and hopped out of the minivan. It felt like we'd just arrived at a farm. There was a large ramshackle building with aluminum siding. Two men stood leaning against a tractor in work overalls.

Next to the building was a trail, and, not really knowing where else to go, we started walking down it. We quickly arrived at a fork, where a signpost indicated that one way was closed: DUE TO ENDANGERED SPECIES NESTING SEASON AND PRESSURES BEING PLACED ON HABITAT, THIS AREA IS CLOSED.

A pine warbler flew by our heads and landed on a branch over the trail in front of us. I pulled out my binoculars to get a closer look.

I felt a tap on my shoulder. It was John. He pointed up—

"Delta Airbus," he said. The plane was coming in to land.

"Thanks, John," I said.

We walked farther in. No woodpeckers yet.

The main reason that the red-cockaded woodpecker is endangered is that it has very specific habitat requirements: the birds can only live in mature longleaf pine forests with no undergrowth.

Want to know how you get a forest to not have undergrowth? Forest fires. The woodpeckers are susceptible to attacks from predators hiding in the understory, and without forest fires, that vegetation builds up.

For the past hundred years, logging has destroyed a lot of the birds' habitat. But, ironically, so has forest fire prevention. The woodpeckers' population has declined to one percent of its original size.

Even W. G. Jones State Forest has to be actively managed, which is what those buildings by the entrance were for. There are regularly prescribed burns to mimic what happens when a forest is struck by lightning and people aren't around to put out the fire.

Habitat isn't the woodpeckers' only peculiarity. They live in big family groups, and they're the only species of woodpecker to nest in living trees. It can take up to six years for them to carve out a nest—and the longest these birds have ever been recorded to live is twelve years. That's like if you got a flat tire when you were eighteen and didn't finish patching it until you were in your mid-fifties.

And then once they finish building a nest, they often don't even get to live in it. They get bullied out of their homes all the time. Pileated woodpeckers will enlarge the entryway so it's too big for the red-cockaded to live in anymore, and over two dozen other species of vertebrates have been documented stealing red-cockaded woodpecker nests. Even insects will live in the holes. The animal kingdom as a whole has decided to walk all over the red-cockaded woodpecker. It's like the fall guy for the entire forest.

As we hiked on, I noticed that the trees were all evenly spaced. I later learned that this wasn't a real old-growth forest—a hundred years ago the land had been a pine seedling nursery, and the trees we were walking through now had actually been planted during the Great Depression.

The woodpeckers had been attracted to the habitat, which just so happened to be the type of forest that stood here before the area was first logged. The birds were an unintended consequence of reseeding the forest.

Another unintended consequence: gay men. Until recently, the W. G. Jones State Forest has been a meet-up spot for gay men to have anonymous sex. The park rangers have struggled for decades to stop people from having sex in the woods and have closed the forest at times to try to curtail the activity.

Anyway, we were just looking for birds.

There was a buzzing in my ears again. I slapped myself in the face. Despite having brought enough DEET-based repellent to bring about the End Times for mosquitoes throughout the region, I was still getting eaten alive.

There were other sounds, too. We could hear the roar of the highway in the distance. Children were playing and yelling at each other in the backyards of the housing development that bordered the forest just a couple of hundred yards away from us. We could see rows of houses through the trees. A jackhammer started up—literally, a jackhammer—and police sirens wailed by.

Yet despite all of the noise and the close proximity to humans, this tiny strip of land was home to one of the largest groups of endangered red-cockaded woodpeckers in the state.

We crept along the trail, binoculars at the ready, stopping at the slightest sound. Joggers and elderly couples from the neighborhood said good morning as they passed by.

Walter spotted a small bird in the uppermost canopy of one of the trees—it was right over our heads, moving rapidly from branch to branch. I finally tracked it down with my binoculars—it looked like a glowing Cheeto.

"That's a Blackburnian warbler," Walter said. "You see the bright orange throat?"

I pulled out my phone and texted Tyler Blackburn to let him know there was a bird named after him.

We kept walking, our eyes turned upward. My neck was getting stiff from looking up for so long, and I was beginning to go cross-eyed from staring into my binoculars.

I turned to Walter: "I keep seeing creases in the bark of trees and thinking it's a bird," I said.

"That's the Matrix," John said, popping up behind us. He skipped down the trail, stopping from time to time to inspect clusters of poison ivy.

Walter looked at his watch. "Let's keep looking for another hour or so. If we can't find it, we'll take John to the Space Center."

Out in front of us, John started to sing an Irish ballad, his voice echoing through the woods. He was clearly bored out of his mind. Walter looked at me, laughed, and rolled his eyes. John was going to scare all the birds away.

I caught up to him and told him to quiet down. He smiled, shrugged, and stopped singing. He pointed at a tree just off the trail.

"What kind of bird is that?" he asked.

I looked to where he was pointing. A fat, feisty-looking mockingbird was perched on one of the lower branches of a pine about forty feet away from us.

"It's nothing. Just a mockingbird," I said.

"Not that one," he said. "*That* one, right there."

He continued to point at the same bird, which had begun to sing loudly, its throat feathers puffing out as it called.

"It's a mockingbird, John. The same kind we have back in Los Angeles."

As I spoke, a small speckled bird with white cheeks flew in and landed on the same branch as the mockingbird, scaring it off. It moved around the limb, grappling onto the bark with its clawed feet.

"That's the bird I meant," John said, clearly full of shit.

Three other woodpeckers swooped down into the tree to join the first one.

"Those birds too," he said. "Those are the ones I meant."

John, with his loud, stomping boots and his half-remembered drinking songs, had somehow found the bird we were looking for.

We stood there, watching in awe, as the small woodpecker family worked its way around the tree. We crept along the trail to get a better view.

The birds were enchanting. They lived in an area surrounded by golf courses and strip malls—habitats most any animal can't survive in.

I turned to the guys:

"I feel a little starstruck," I said.

"What do you mean?" Walter asked.

"I'm not sure, exactly," I said.

I thought about it as we walked along. For me, finding this woodpecker—even just getting the chance to see it—felt special. Up until that point, I had only seen it in pictures, and here I was now seeing it in the wild.

Eventually the woodpeckers disappeared. We could have turned back, but we decided to push on. We crossed a swinging rope bridge and walked along a creek that was saturated with water moccasins. I counted six of them. The previous day we'd seen more birders than birds. Today we saw more venomous snakes.

We continued walking down an increasingly overgrown path. It didn't seem like we were going the right way. Suddenly the trees parted and we were spit out onto the shoulder of the highway. Eighteen-wheelers honked as they blew by. The sun was beating down and it was getting hot. It was time to head back to Houston.

The next morning we flew back to Los Angeles, and I got back just in time to make it to a table read for the next episode of *PLL*.

That night, lying in my own bed for the first time in days, Sophia and the dogs by my side, something felt off. I couldn't fall asleep. I kept thinking about that tiny forest just outside of Houston.

I closed my eyes, and I could see the woodpeckers again. A few small birds, holding on to the last acres that can support them in this world, because that's all they have left, a scatter plot of managed forests spread across the South. Their world is gone. And what they have left can barely support what remains of their population.

I thought about what it must feel like to be a part of a dying species. To have lost everything that resembles your original "home" and to have your body somehow, instinctually, recognize that.

Part of what I feel as a birder is a sense of urgency. Habitats are disappearing at a sprinter's pace all around the world.

Often, when I see a rare bird for the first time, I know it may also be my last.

I feel lucky to have seen a red-cockaded woodpecker—I know there's a good chance I won't see one again.

## PUT YOUR BEST

## FEATHER FORWARD

In polite society it's considered taboo to wear white after Labor Day. In the birding community, it's considered taboo to wear white ever.

The color white scares birds away—or so the argument goes—because it's hardly ever found in nature. Red hats or neon-colored sneakers are always acceptable to wear when you're out in the woods, but a good pair of white chinos is a total birding fashion faux pas.

The story I've heard is that the whole "never wear white" rule started when some ornithologist disturbed a rare bird at its nest while he was wearing a white shirt. Frankly, I think he just got too close to the bird and his presence made it uncomfortable. But the guy was wearing white at the time, so now nobody can.

This is, of course, ridiculous, but it's one of those ideas that gets ingrained in a community and then goes unquestioned. Like how actors superstitiously say "break a leg" instead of "good luck," or how they'll never say the word "Macbeth" in a theater.

Really, it's okay to wear white after Labor Day, and it's okay to wear white while birding. (Still, you probably shouldn't say "Macbeth" in a theater.)

A few years ago my girlfriend and I took a vacation to Paris that happened to coincide with Fashion Week, and we received an invitation to attend a Giorgio Armani runway show. I was told that the event would be dressy, and my birding sense of fashion took "dressy" to mean "no white shirts allowed." So I wore all black.

The Armani event was filled with the most insanely trendy people, and Sophia and I had to be careful not to openly stare. Some of the clothing looked like bird-of-paradise mating plumages.

Walking to my seat for the runway show, I passed by actors whom I'd admired for years. Kristin Scott Thomas, Robin Wright, Ben Foster. Seated across the catwalk from me was Anna Wintour.

The show began, and the runway models began their walk. I leaned over to the model sitting next to me and whispered, "What do you think the most common injury in runway modeling is?"

Without missing a beat, she said, "Look at their feet."

Every other woman's toes stuck out over the front of her open-toed shoes, or arched in some anatomically impossible way. My seatmate explained that most shoes in runway shows are sample size, and thus don't often fit the larger-than-normal size feet of models.

After the show, I was ushered backstage to meet Papa Giorgio, the legend himself. He was exceptionally kind, and spoke to me in Italian. I love the sound of the language, as you know, but I don't speak a word of it.

Giorgio looked at me and said "*bello*" a few times. I turned to his niece, who stood next to him. She grinned and said, "He says you're very ugly."

"Tell him I come from a long line of ugly men," I said. Papa Giorgio nodded solemnly.

On my way out of the event, I passed by Juliette Binoche. We made eye contact for the briefest of moments, and she smiled. I smiled back, concentrating all my attention on my knees. I was worried that they might give out in her presence. I've had a crush on her since I was a little kid.

Outside, paparazzi were milling about. One looked up at me from his phone for a moment, then looked back down. Angry Birds was clearly more important. I walked down a flight of stairs and made my way to a car that was waiting.

Right before I reached the car, a young woman broke from the crowd that had gathered outside the event and walked up to me. She asked if she could take a photo, and I said of course. She beckoned several friends over, and one of them shrieked with glee.

The paparazzo who had been playing Angry Birds was the first to look up, but the shriek caught all of their attention. The sleeping photographers we'd passed on the stairs came to life and descended like a wake of vultures. I didn't even get a chance to take a photo with the group of fans. Machine gun–like camera flashes went off as the paparazzi swarmed. "Yan! Yan!" they called out, shouting the French pronunciation of my name.

We smiled for the cameras as we stepped backward to our waiting car and leapt in.

As an actor and an artist, I deeply respect the fashion world and its eccentricities. As a birder, I have no idea what the hell fashion is all about.

Birders don't care much about fashion. The "no white" rule is the closest thing we have to a line in the sand, and it's a blurry line. Birding fashion is pretty laissez-faire. It's mostly earth tones and muted grays. Some people wear nylon fishing shirts and cargo shorts; the very serious wear camouflage. The only real constants in the world of birding fashion are probably our wide-brimmed hats and orthopedic inserts.

Birders aren't fashion people. If anything, we're gear people.

For a hobby that only really requires eyes and ears to enjoy—and for some just one of those senses—people can get pretty into their gear.

Binoculars are the most obvious calling card of a birder and the only major piece of equipment one needs to get started. Some people wear them proudly around their necks, with ergonomic back straps that keep them from bouncing when they need to walk briskly. Other people palm their binoculars and hold them at their sides, hoping strangers don't think they're Peeping Toms as they walk around the Silver Lake Reservoir at 6:00 A.M.

More serious birders will also invest in a spotting scope, which is basically a miniature telescope designed for looking at birds. Scopes were initially used by hunters to spot game, and by soldiers to spot the enemy. They have stronger magnification than binoculars but are harder to use. Scopes have to be mounted to something like a tripod to keep the image steady, so they're best for watching birds that don't move too much.

Some people take it a step further and get really into bird photography. There are lens attachments that connect cameras to spotting scopes—a type of photography called "digiscoping."

Bird photography is the most gear-intensive variation of birding. I tried to do a little bird photography right after I got back into birding, and one time I got a couple of decent shots of geese by holding my iPhone up to a spotting scope.

But the truth is, it's just not for me. I always feel like the camera separates me from what I'm looking at. That I'm never actually seeing what's right in front of me—it just becomes an image on a screen.

Nowadays, I only bring binoculars with me when I go out birding.

People who get really into bird photography remind me of paparazzi.

A few years back, a rare-bird alert went out for a varied bunting—a tiny red-and-purple songbird not normally found in the LA area. I had the day off from shooting, so I drove out to the park in Duarte where the bird had been spotted.

I arrived to find a flock of bird photographers with their camera kits—camouflaged telephoto lenses, tripods, monopods, the whole nine yards.

One guy was standing at the trunk of his car, changing out the lenses on his DSLR. He pulled an enormous white telephoto lens out of a camera bag.

Aside from the fact that it was white—why risk scaring the birds away?—it was the exact same lens I'd seen paparazzi carry around to take sneaky candid shots of celebrities—the ones where they're looking fat at the beach, fighting on hotel balconies, getting Starbucks in sweatpants, and so on.

In Paris, all of the paparazzi I'd seen had carried smaller, more compact lenses. Those photographers were lining the red carpet—they didn't need telephoto lenses to capture their subjects, who were generally willing to be photographed anyway. The big white lenses I'm talking about serve a different purpose.

Two years before, I'd seen the same type of lens when I was leaving my costar Lucy's birthday party. We'd gone to a restaurant called Beso in Hollywood. As we were waiting for our cars at the valet stand, I noticed a man across the street surreptitiously photographing us from behind a Dumpster. The streetlight above him illuminated his white telephoto lens, giving him away immediately as a paparazzo.

It felt like an intrusion. It's always nice when fans come up to say hi. It's not always nice being photographed from behind a Dumpster—it makes you feel like a Cold War spy whose cover has just been blown.

I wonder if birds feel the same way about having their picture taken.

# REHAB

A lot of people who work in entertainment end up in rehab at some point. Drugs, alcohol, anxiety—there are countless reasons to go. I've only been to rehab once so far, and it was just for an afternoon. Also, it was for birds.

As is often the case with this sort of thing, it all started with a party. A few years back, I went to a fund-raiser for the Humane Society in Beverly Hills. My costar Torrey DeVitto had invited me to tag along. Torrey does a lot of volunteer work with animal rehabilitation and is a big animal rights activist. She's also a vegan—I think. I'm pretty sure she is. Every time she comes over for dinner I only cook vegetables, so either she's a vegan or she's convinced that I am. I should actually ask her about that.

Fund-raisers and galas are a pretty big staple in the Hollywood calendar. They bring together celebs and causes to raise money and get the word out about important issues. Whenever I attend one of these events, I spend most of my time by the buffet table. I've never shaken the poor-college-student mentality out of my head, so if there's free food, I stock up.

I'm not always the most graceful of birds at these Hollywood parties. A few years ago, I was invited to a scotch tasting. After I'd tried a number of different scotches, I got cornered by a stockbroker who was complaining that the party wasn't extravagant enough. I excused myself as politely as I could.

In the next room I found a chair and had a seat. It was made of white marble and was incredibly cool to the touch. It felt less like a chair than it did a piece of art, which was interesting, because that's exactly what it was: art. A worried personal assistant soon informed me that I was sitting on one of the host's priceless new acquisitions.

But I've gotten off topic. Back to the Humane Society party: I was standing across the room from Torrey, eating oysters at the buffet table, when a woman came up and introduced herself as Yvonne Bennett. We started chatting, and I found out that Yvonne worked with the Humane Society.

The Humane Society has always had a special place in my heart, and I told Yvonne as much. Growing up, my mom would take my sister and me to visit the cats and dogs up for adoption as an after-school activity.

"That's wonderful," Yvonne said. "Thankfully dog adoptions have gone up over the past few years. But there are certain animals that are hard to get folks to care about."

"Like what?"

"Well, birds, for instance."

"Oh, really? Like, pigeons?"

She laughed.

"No, a lot of what we do involves rehabilitating wild animals and then releasing them back into the wild once they're better. But birds aren't cute. People don't flip out for rehabilitated falcons like they do for Dalmatian puppies. There just isn't much of an interest in it. Bird rehab to most people is just 'boring but important' work."

I had my hand to my mouth and was midway through slurping down another oyster when she said this.

"You rehabilitate falcons?" I asked, oyster still in my mouth.

"Falcons, hawks, herons, you name it. We have a red-tailed hawk we're due to release next week down in Ramona."

I was coughing, choking on the oyster in excitement.

I love hawks. Birds of prey in general are pretty awesome—I've been obsessed with them ever since Mr. Hawkins, that red-tailed hawk that lived near my house when I was a kid.

I asked Yvonne if I could come along to see the red-tailed hawk when they released it. Of course, she said. And, as it turned out, my possibly vegan costar Torrey was going to be there, too.

Thinking back on it now, I wonder if Torrey had tipped off Yvonne about my love of birds.

The next Saturday, Torrey and I piled into my station wagon and drove to Ramona, California. If I haven't said it enough already, I was very excited. I'd been in Los Angeles for half a decade, and here I was just now learning that there were regular releases of wild birds of prey. What the hell had I been doing with my weekends?

We met Yvonne at a rehabilitation facility called the Fund

for Animals Wildlife Center. Yvonne and Ali Crumpacker came out to greet us in the parking lot when we arrived. Ali is the director of the animal rehab center in Ramona. Her general demeanor reminded me of Robert Muldoon—the raptor-obsessed game warden from the original *Jurassic Park*. Before moving to Southern California, she spent twelve years tracking lions in South Africa.

Ali was warm and welcoming, but it was clear that she wasn't particularly interested in photo ops. If you were at the Wildlife Center, you were there to work. And work we did.

The first thing we did was chop up frozen mice carcasses to feed to a couple of crows that were being treated at the center. We hadn't had coffee yet, and already we were chopping off mouse heads. A volunteer showed us her tried-and-true method for efficiently dismembering them.

We fed the mice to the crows and then headed over to the main animal holding area. By the entrance was a massive floor-to-ceiling whiteboard. A grid was drawn on the board—each box in the grid represented a cage, and a number was written inside each of the boxes. The numbers were followed by letters: initials to denote species.

One of the boxes had WSO written after the numbers. I decided to hazard a guess.

"Is that one a western screech owl?" I said, pointing.

Ali nodded. "We got him in a few days ago. He's still in quarantine or I'd let you see him."

"What do the numbers mean?"

Ali smiled. "All of the animals here are numbered. It helps us resist the urge to name them." She pushed open the door, and we stepped into the enclosure. On each side of us were pens holding injured animals. Mountain lions that had eaten rat poison, bobcats that had stepped into traps, abandoned baby skunks that were so cute it hurt to look at them.

We passed a cage with a kiddie pool inside it—there was a pygmy hippo splashing about in the water. Yvonne said they'd rescued the hippo from Beverly Hills. Some millionaire's idea of a funny gift for his kid.

As we walked, Ali explained the volunteers' relationship with the animals. "We're all here because we love animals, of course, but sometimes that's the problem. A lot of these animals are here because they got too close to humans. They weren't properly afraid of us. People want to nurse sick animals back to health, but that can actually be really bad for them. The last thing we want is for the injured animal to imprint on us. We're here to help them be independent again. So no names, just numbers. We try to touch them as little as possible, and our attendants are instructed not to talk to them either. We're like ghosts."

"Is that hard?" I asked. "What's it like being surrounded by animals and having to actively ignore them?"

Ali's response came quickly, almost like a mantra. She'd had to answer questions like this countless times. "Part of loving animals—truly loving them—is caring about what's best for them. Often that means removing yourself from the equation."

The red-tailed hawk we were going to be releasing wasn't in the main enclosure. He'd already been transferred to a separate holding area to get him ready for his transition back to the wild. We hopped into a couple of Jeeps and drove out to the field to meet him.

A handful of volunteers were standing in the field. On a table, there was a small blue box—about two feet long and eight inches wide. Judging by the wide berth everyone was giving this blue box, it was clear that the hawk was inside.

As we pulled into the field, Yvonne turned around in the front seat to face me. "So what do you think, Ian?" she said. "Want to release it by yourself?"

I froze. I must have been smiling because Ali glanced at me in the rearview mirror then let out a deep guffaw. Yes. Yes, I wanted to release it. Holy shit, yes.

Then a thought ran through my head. This might all be an elaborate prank—and I'd been pranked before.

A couple of years ago, my costar Lucy fooled the hell out of me. She knew I was really into street art, and she convinced me that she had a connection to Banksy—the famously anonymous graffiti artist. She asked me if I wanted to meet him, and I jumped at the opportunity.

Lucy took me to a parking lot late one night to meet him. I tried to play it cool, doing my best not to let on how excited I was.

It turned out the whole thing was an episode for the show *Punk'd*. I fell for it, hook, line, and sinker.

Sitting in the car now, out in this field on a wildlife preserve, my mind flashed back to that night in the parking lot. I turned to look at Torrey. Was Torrey pranking me right now? Would she do such a thing? With Lucy I'd totally expect it. But Torrey isn't like that. Torrey likes classical music and nature conservatories. But could I be sure of that?

I swallowed and turned back to Yvonne. I nodded. "Yes, please."

"Cool," she said, and we got out of the car.

This wasn't a prank. This was real.

Ali informed one of the attendants that I would be releasing the hawk. He came over and showed me how to handle the little blue box. Hold it at arm's length, he said, with the door tilted away from your body. Then kneel down low, tilt the door toward the ground, and pull this switch to open it.

"The hawk will do all the rest," he told me. "You just hold on tight."

We went over to the table, where Ali was holding the box.

"Have fun," she said and handed it to me.

As I walked out into the open field, the hawk started to rustle inside the box. I glanced through one of the slats on top. A single, massive pupil stared back at me.

The hawk stopped moving. It opened and closed its beak silently.

A couple of months back, the bird had been brought to the shelter after it flew into a power line. Its wing had been badly scorched. It had taken weeks just to get it to move its wing again. But now it was strong. Strong and hungry.

The hawk hadn't been fed that day. They wanted it to be hungry when it was released so that it would immediately fly off to hunt. It was eyeing me like I was food.

I knelt in the middle of the field, holding the box out at arm's length. I angled the door down and away from me. I turned back to look at the small crowd waiting expectantly back by the cars. Torrey gave me an enthusiastic thumbs-up. I waved, took a deep breath, and turned back to the box. I steadied myself, making sure that I had a firm grip. I grabbed the switch, pulled it, and felt the door swing open.

Nothing happened.

The hawk didn't budge. Not even a little bit. It just sat there, at the bottom of the box. I could see the sunlight hitting his beak, illuminating its razor-sharp edges.

I looked back at the crowd of attendants. Nobody moved.

I turned back to the hawk. I tilted the box a little higher and gave it a light shake. This immediately seemed like a bad idea. Who shakes a hawk?

The bird remained where it was, refusing to move an inch.

At that point, curiosity got the best of me. Like Elmer Fudd with a jammed rifle, I lifted up the box and turned the door to face me. The red-tailed hawk and I stared at each other, his face not two feet from mine.

I blinked. The hawk didn't.

Then it let out a bloodcurdling shriek.

I don't know if any of you have ever heard a red-tailed hawk shriek. Actually, I take that back. You definitely have. If you've ever seen a movie that has a bald eagle in it, you've heard a red-tailed hawk. Actual eagles sound like they're whimpering, so, in Hollywood, eagles are always dubbed over with the sound of red-tailed hawk screeches.

It's a majestic and inspiring sound. Unless it's inches from your face. Which this was.

The hawk pushed its feet against the box and rocketed out toward me. Its wings brushed my hair, and it flew out low over the field, flapping to try and gain altitude. I ran back to join the crowd around the table.

The hawk flew about a hundred feet then crash-landed into the brambles at the far end of the field. It stayed there, staring at us. We all stared back.

Then Ali let out a growl. She set off sprinting toward the hawk, arms waving, yelling.

Torrey leaned over and whispered into my ear: "This is always the hardest part for me. They have to scare him away. He still thinks they're going to feed him his dinner."

The hawk looked dazed. It stared at Ali as if confused. She picked up a clod of dirt from the ground and tossed it in the bird's direction. As the dirt landed, the hawk spread its wings and took flight, disappearing over a stand of eucalyptus trees.

Ali slowly walked back to join us, wiping the dirt from her hands on her khaki shorts.

"That's so sad," I said to Torrey. Ali heard me. She smiled and shook her head.

"It's the only way. If we did our jobs right he won't ever see us again. There are no warm goodbyes in this line of work."

# LIFE IN

# THE WINGS

Probably the least "Hollywood" part of my life as an actor is actually being on set. The press junkets and the parties can be glamorous, but when we're shooting *Pretty Little Liars*, I wake up and drive to work every morning just like most people.

Sometimes work starts early. If my call time is at 6:00 A.M.— which it is if I'm in the first scene of the day—I set my alarm for 5:07. Even though I wouldn't call myself a superstitious man, seven is my lucky number, and I believe in starting the day off right.

I'm usually the first actor to arrive on set. I grew up in a military family, and I inherited my dad's deep, almost panicky respect for punctuality. He believes that unless you are liter-ally caught behind enemy lines, you need to be on time.

Two seasons ago the producers installed a shower in my dressing room. Originally, I thought it was a gift, but then Lucy told me it was put in because I always smelled really bad. I like to think she was kidding, but either way, I make sure to take a shower before work. I almost always use my on-set shower instead of the one at home, because I don't want to wake up Sophia or the dogs.

After I get cleaned up, I usually eat breakfast on set. There's a craft services room at the back of one of the soundstages, complete with an unlimited supply of bacon. Most of the cast and crew stop by in the morning, and it's where I usually run into people at the beginning of the day.

The person I run into most often here is Troian Bellisario, who plays Spencer on the show. Troian, like me, is compulsively early. She's constantly moving and constantly working. She's an actor, yes, but she also writes, produces, and directs. She even directed a recent episode of the show. It's fortunate that she isn't evil—otherwise she'd easily take over the world. In the meantime, she makes a great breakfast buddy.

The only time us actors avoid craft services is when we have to shoot a sex scene. On those days, you'll find me drinking coffee and doing push-ups in my dressing room. When it's a sex-scene day, we'll all avoid craft services so that we look nice and svelte when the cameras start rolling. All of us, that is, except for Keegan, who walks around eating entire pizzas before he has to take off his shirt.

Around my third plate of bacon—it'd be a shame to let it all go to waste—I'll usually get a text from Lisa Hoggett, the set PA, telling me to get my ass over to hair and makeup. I'll grab an apple on my way out so I at least keep up the appearance of making healthy choices.

Hair and makeup is in one of several trailers set up between the sound stages. We call this area "base camp."

On my way over, I'll stop by the PA trailer to say good morning to Matt Buckler. Matt and I have been affectionately trading insults on a daily basis for several years. He and his wife are both lovely. (She had a guest spot in a recent episode of *PLL*.) Matt makes sure all the actors have their sides for the day.

"Sides" are a compact version of whichever parts of the script we're shooting that day, and each actor gets sides for just the scenes they're in. We have to review them carefully: there are often last-minute edits and revisions to the version of the script we were sent the week before.

Sides are handed out every morning, then collected again at the end of the day. The producers are strict about this because the episodes have to remain secret until they air on TV. Nobody wants even the smallest of plotlines leaked. At the end of each shoot day, we hand our sides over to Lisa, and she promptly destroys them. If we ever accidentally took them home with us, I am confident that Lisa would hunt us down à la *Rambo: First Blood*.

Once I get my sides from Matt, I'll quickly read through them to refresh my memory and see if there are any new lines I need to memorize, then walk up the steps to the hair and makeup trailer.

Inside, the first person I visit is Cindy Miguens, who's in charge of the hair and makeup department. Cindy sits me down, closely examines my face, asks me why I can't take better care of my skin, then proceeds to cover my face with a hot towel before I can answer.

Cindy says the towel is good for my pores, but I can't help but think she might just be trying to smother me. I regifted the

NutriBullet she gave me for my birthday a couple years back, and she's never let me live it down. In my defense, I gave the NutriBullet to my mom, so I still use it every time I go visit her. It's still in the family.

Also, Cindy and I share the same birthday, September sixteenth. Apparently we were both conceived after Christmas parties.

Not long after I regifted the NutriBullet, Cindy was planning a whitewater rafting trip, so I gave her a small plastic travel potty. She now uses it as a container to grow herbs in her backyard. I regifted, she repurposed—it all evens out.

After the hot towel, Cindy shaves my stubble to whatever length it needs to be that day. It's a little embarrassing, but I'm not allowed to shave myself. If I happened to nick my face, it could delay the shoot and cost the studio a lot of money. I'm not about to put up a fight on this rule, though: I've been shaving my own face for well over a decade, and I still haven't gotten the hang of it.

After the shave, Cindy puts on makeup to hide any blemishes and make my skin look like I've never had a zit before. Around this time, the coffee kicks in and I (a) wake up, and (b) start sweating, which is my natural state of being. Cindy sighs and begins to powder my face so that I don't sweat off all her hard work.

On mornings when Cindy is working on one of the other actors or actresses, I'll go over to Rebecca Wachtel-Herrera for my makeup instead. Rebecca is extremely efficient. She has a lot of people to get through each morning, usually in quick succession, so she's really good at getting people in and out of the seat quickly. She knows that I am really, really bad about sitting still—I constantly turn my head back and forth to take part in different conversations, and I'll say hi to anyone who walks in—so Rebecca has perfected the art of applying makeup to a moving target.

Also, her husband, Christian, is a fellow bird lover. Once, when I was over at their house for dinner, Christian and I saw a pair of red-whiskered bulbuls fly through their backyard. Red-whiskered bulbuls normally live in Asia, but there's an established population here in Los Angeles, which probably got its start from a handful of escaped pet birds. We sat around outside for half an hour, waiting for the birds to come back, completely forgetting about the food we'd left on the grill.

For hair, I either go to Kim Ferry or Valentino Agundez. My hair naturally forms into a tangled bird's nest, like Jonah Hill's in *Superbad*, so there's a fair amount of taming that needs to be done before they'll put me in front of a camera.

Kim is like a ninja with a straightening iron. I'll be horsing around with Shay or Troian and won't even notice Kim working. All of a sudden, she'll say, "Done," and I'll look up and my hair will be perfect.

If Kim's working on someone else, I'll go to Valentino's station at the far end of the trailer. Her chair is up in a raised side room—it's like a tree house. Valentino and I could talk for hours if they'd let us. We'll go on about everything from our dreams to race relations in America to whether or not humans will ever evolve to lose their pinky toes. It's hard to sit still when I'm talking to her, and I often end up jumping out of the chair to demonstrate a point or act out part of a story.

Once hair and makeup are done, I head to set. We film in the soundstages around base camp, and walking onto the stage

I'll often bump into the head of electric, Eric Forand, also known as E4. I'll say hey to E4 and also to the assistant director, who is almost always around. It varies from episode to episode, so the AD will either be Arthur Anderson, Jenn Anderson, or Laura Sylvestor. The Andersons aren't related.

At this point, we'll do a quick rehearsal of the scene we're about to film. Depending on who the director is—almost every episode has a different director—the rehearsal might be a full run-through of the scene, or it might just be blocking to figure out where we'll be sitting or standing in relation to the camera. Once we all feel like we've got a solid grasp on the scene, the actors are excused from set and they call in our stand-ins.

Tyler Maskell has been my stand-in for years. I pester him, and he plays along, sometimes feigning tears from all the abuse I give him.

The stand-ins are brought in so that the crew can adjust the lights and camera and set pieces around them. When I first started filming the show, I tried to help out. One time, the director said, "We need that lamp moved six inches to the right," and I was standing nearby, so I reached over and moved the lamp six inches to the right. I should've been yelled at, but a producer was nice enough to pull me aside and explain that actors aren't allowed to touch set pieces. It's against union rules. If I try and help out, I could get somebody fired. In college I worked crew on shows all the time, and the "don't help anyone" rule took some serious getting used to.

After the stand-ins are brought in, I'll often swing by Video Village to chat with the writers. Video Village is a collection of chairs and monitors set up directly next to wherever we happen to be shooting. Writers and producers gather there so they can watch the scenes as they're being filmed without bumping into set pieces or peering over the director's shoulder.

The writers on *PLL* are fantastic. They've juggled dozens of storylines over seven seasons. On top of that, they always make themselves available to us, and are willing to answer any questions we might have about the scenes we're shooting that day. There's rarely any improvising on the show, but the writers are open to word or line changes if we've got a solid argument for them.

When lighting and sound are ready to roll, Lucy and I head to stage and find our marks. I say Lucy because, as her on-screen love interest, most of my scenes are with her. Sometimes we'll rehearse again with lighting and sound in place, but we'll usually film the rehearsal. We try to be as efficient as possible with our scenes because we know everyone has families or other things to get to. We've learned that being overly precious with a scene doesn't help the performance—it just takes up time people could be spending with their kids.

Lucy is number one on the call sheet, and I'm number seven—told you it was my lucky number. Lucy's higher placement means she has some say in how we shoot the scenes.

After we've filmed the wide-angle "master"—the shot where you can see both actors at once—we move on to individual coverage, which is basically the same thing as a close-up on one actor. Traditionally, whoever is higher on the call sheet gets to decide if they'd like to go first or second, so they get to either prepare during the other actor's takes, or go first while everything is still fresh. Lucy never seems to care about going first or second, unless it's for a highly dramatic scene that she's the main focus of.

On some productions, after the actor with the higher number on the call sheet finishes their coverage, they'll leave set. This means that their scene partner is left to act opposite a PA with a script in their hand.

This bit of set politics has never been an issue on our show. Lucy has only left set during my coverage once before, and it was because we were running late and she had to hop on a plane for a family emergency. Her focus has always been on whatever makes the day run smoothly.

After we finish a scene and are excused from set, Lucy will always find a place to curl up and take a nap. The girl naps everywhere. She could sleep on a bed made of barbed wire if she wanted to.

If I've got a bit of a break between scenes and need some rest, I'll usually head back to my dressing room.

Shortly after we started work on season four, Marlene King—the showrunner and executive producer of *PLL*—was walking by my dressing room and poked her head in. She took a look around and I think assumed that I was horribly depressed based on the room's general lack of style and cleanliness. I'd never thought about decorating the place, and I'd let it get pretty messy. Marlene was worried, so she had the room redecorated with bright colors, put some art on the walls, and even got me a new mini fridge.

The new décor was actually pretty nice, but the fridge didn't last long. One day I walked in to find Shay Mitchell—who plays Emily on the show—stealing it. When I caught her red-handed, she began to laugh maniacally.

"Don't just stand there, Ian. Help me get this over to my dressing room," she said. I proceeded to help her steal my own fridge.

Shay also regularly takes food that I'm eating right out of my hands and eats it in front of me. She's basically the little sister I never had—the little sister who expresses love through torment.

If I see Ashley Benson, who plays Hanna, I'll pretend to hide. Not a day has gone by when she hasn't tried to punch me in the balls. It's a game we've been playing since season one. Ashley's a good friend, and she'll periodically steal my dogs and take them on adventures.

After we've been on set for six hours, we are released for "lunch." I put lunch in quotation marks because it's not a time-of-day-sensitive meal. When we have night shoots, we'll have a lunch break at two in the morning.

We had one of those nighttime lunch breaks when we were shooting the noir episode at the end of season four. Keegan and I were excused a little early for our lunch break, around 8:30 P.M., and we decided to leave the lot for dinner.

Across the street from where we film is a place called the Smoke House, an old Hollywood watering hole that's been serving actors from the Warner Bros. lot since the forties. We rolled up in costumes that would've fit right in back when the restaurant was founded—Keegan looked like a young Dick Tracy.

The waiter seated us at George Clooney's table—he was a regular at the Smoke House back in his *ER* days—and we sat there, sipping dirty martinis, eating heaping bowls of pasta. I don't usually go in much for Hollywood nostalgia, but it was a memorable lunch.

Similar to how "lunch" is a multiuse term, whenever I finish shooting all of my coverage, no matter what time of day it is, the AD will shout, "That's a goodnight to Ian!" and then everyone on set will call out goodnight. I've been wished a sincere goodnight at both three in the morning and three in the afternoon.

Before leaving set, we hang up our clothes—you don't want any enemies, especially in the costume department—then grab our bags and head out.

Sometimes I'll grab a small to-go box of bacon for the road.

## NO MORE DUCK

## FOR BAILEY

A few years ago, Sophia and I were driving to meet up with a friend for lunch on Wilshire Boulevard. We were running pretty early.

Driving past the La Brea Tar Pits, I noticed that No-Kill Los Angeles, a group that promotes adoption of dogs and cats, was having its annual pet adoption weekend on the park grounds.

When I first moved to Los Angeles, I'd lived practically across the street from the tar pits, and I'd visited the event then. I hadn't seriously considered adopting at the time because my apartment didn't allow dogs—and I didn't have the space.

We had a half hour to spare before lunch, and we decided to stop and look at some of the animals.

Walking up and down the rows of white tents that had been set up to shade the kennels, I found myself thinking about how all these animals ended up here. Families who got evicted and couldn't afford to keep their beloved pets. Nine-year-old ex-fighting dogs. Puppies who proved too energetic for their owners' patience.

The cages were filled with beautiful animals—some friendly, others clearly frightened. It all started to get to me—so many cats and dogs find new, loving homes at these adoption fairs, but then you also know not every animal will be so lucky.

Around the corner of one of the rows of tents, there was a small crowd gathered around a kennel. Suddenly, Sophia let out a yelp and sprinted ahead. She disappeared into the crowd. I squeezed apologetically through several rows of shoulders and elbows to get to the front and catch up with her. When I finally got to where she was standing, Sophia was grinning from ear to ear. She pointed at a kennel. Inside were two labradoodles: Mochi, a girl, and Bailey, her brother.

Mochi was the smaller of the two, with slate gray fur and a chubby face. Bailey was lean and lighter in color, and he had a thin mustache that curled over his upper lip.

Mochi peered from face to face, like she was looking for someone. Her brother was skittishly cowering in a corner, looking over his shoulder to make sure he wasn't about to be surprised from behind.

A girl put her hand up to the metal bars of the kennel to say hi. Bailey, tail between his legs, sidestepped to the opposite corner of the enclosure.

I squatted down next to the kennel and put my hand out. Sophia did the same. Bailey looked over. He cautiously walked over and sat down next to me. He looked up, and we made eye contact. He lowered his head and nuzzled my hand. Mochi wagged her way over to her brother's side and began to lick Sophia's hand through the cage.

At that moment I realized two things: (1) we were getting these dogs, and (2) we were definitely going to be late for lunch.

Sophia agreed to stay with the dogs while I went to find someone who could help us. The adoption counter was in the tent next door, and as I walked over, I heard a man arguing with one of the volunteers. He was trying to adopt Mochi but didn't want to take her brother. The volunteer explained that the dogs were littermates—they hadn't been separated since birth. Ideally, they were looking to find them a home together.

The man took out his wallet and offered to pay extra for Mochi. The volunteer explained that the adoption fee was a set rate, and that they weren't trying to make a profit on the dogs.

Adrenaline took over: "I'll take them both!" I found myself calling out.

The man turned to me.

"I'm adopting the girl now," he said.

"You're offering to buy one, but I'd take them both," I said. I'd only just met them two minutes ago but already I felt protective of these pups.

The volunteer smiled at me—and I knew that we were going to be taking them home.

This was all very unexpected. We'd been on our way to lunch, debating what to do with the rest of our afternoon—and now we had dogs. Plural.

After filling out the paperwork, the volunteer and I walked back to the kennel. She opened the gate and put the dogs on leashes so we could take them to the car. Mochi and Bailey bolted from the enclosure and jumped at Sophia and me. I was wearing a baseball hat, and as I bent down to pet them, Mochi nabbed it off my head, wagging and smiling as she held it in her mouth.

That night the dogs slept in bed with us. I think we may have even shared a pillow.

The next morning they ate a pair of my dress shoes and Bailey threw up in the kitchen.

It's been four years now, and the pups still haven't slept a night apart.

Last year Sophia was spending the holidays with her folks in Florida, so I had the days between Christmas and New Year's all to myself. Los Angeles is especially quiet then—people get together with family, or run from them, fleeing to the mountains or the beach.

The whole town seems to draw its curtains.

The day after Christmas, I was wandering around the house in my boxers trying to find something to do. I'd realphabetized the books on my bookshelf and researched a scuba-diving certification course but didn't sign up for it. I was too restless to commit to anything.

Mochi and Bailey were following me from room to room, clearly frustrated that they hadn't been taken outside yet. I was too lazy to walk them but too lazy to sit still, and they stared at me like I was a sort of inept Judas: the look on their faces less of betrayal than disappointment.

I realized that I couldn't do much more loafing around at

home. I needed to get outside—to get some sunlight and fresh air before the short winter day ran out. I had cabin fever. We all had cabin fever.

I asked the dogs if they wanted to go for a hike. At the sound of the word, Mochi began to sneeze with excitement. She started doing laps around the kitchen island. Bailey ran over to the front door, crying to be let outside.

I loaded them in the car. They ride shotgun—I never said they weren't total divas.

One of the set designers on *Pretty Little Liars* had told me about a hike over in Franklin Canyon that I'd been meaning to explore, so I plugged the location into my phone for directions and set off.

I made my way over to Beverly Hills, and drove up through block after block of almost comically palatial mansions, many of them hidden from the street by towering, multistory hedgerows and security gates. I made a right turn into the park, and suddenly the houses were all behind us.

As I followed a narrow, winding canyon road up into the park, an elderly couple passed by going the opposite direction on a tandem mountain bike—apparently that's a thing people do.

The temperature was dropping outside—it was a whole different microclimate up here. Like a national park had unexpectedly sprung up in the middle of super-fancy suburban Los Angeles.

I passed a sign: COMPLIANCE WITH UPCOMING STOP SIGN SUBJECT TO VIDEO MONITORING AND ENFORCEMENT. And just in case I didn't understand the implications of that sign, another immediately after it stated: PHOTO ENFORCED. Then, a few yards after that, a pedestrian crossing sign.

Franklin Canyon takes its signs very seriously.

I finally got to the stop sign, and after coming to a complete stop and counting to five in my head, I drove around to the right of a small reservoir. It's an idyllic spot, and you may have even seen it before without knowing it: this is where a very young Ron Howard—who at the time went by Ronny—threw a stone into the water in the opening credits of *The Andy Griffith Show*.

The parking lot is at the top of the reservoir. I parked and let the dogs out to do some preliminary sniffing and marking of territory. In the trees above us, a pair of yellow-rumped warblers chased each other in circles.

After poking around a bit, I found a trail that ran along the side of the lake. I took the counterclockwise route, letting the dogs pull me, waiting on them when they found a good scent to work on.

The dogs pulled me over to a small pond filled with mallards and wood ducks. Turtles basked on mossy logs, warming themselves in the oblique winter sunlight. A family with twin girls in matching pink parkas was feeding bread to the ducks—next to a sign forbidding it.

On the far side of the reservoir from the parking lot the trees and reeds along the shore opened up, and I got a great view back over the water. As I walked along, a bird flew in and landed clumsily on the water, skidding to a halt. A wigeon, or maybe a coot.

I thought I'd get a closer look, but juggling my binoculars with one hand while the dogs pulled against the leashes in my other proved impossible. I finally got the dogs to sit.

I scanned the lake again. The duck was still there: a male

hooded merganser! It swam in little loops, the extravagant white crest on its black head fully extended. Beady yellow eyes unblinking. I guessed there was a female around nearby— probably somewhere just out of sight.

And there she was, coming out of the brush hanging over the edge of the lake.

Mergansers have a special place in my heart. It was that hooded merganser at Big Bear that brought me back into birding as an adult. Seeing the pair of them now, I felt my mind begin to relax. The postholiday stress and tension started to melt away.

And then something weird happened. Watching the two little ducks on the reservoir, Mochi and Bailey patiently tolerating my love of birds, a strange feeling crept up on me. It was a feeling I hadn't experienced while birding before, and also one that I haven't since. I was very hungry—starving, in fact.

And what I craved at that moment, more than anything in the world, was duck.

We didn't dawdle on the way back to the car. Hike finished, dogs loaded up, my hat in Mochi's mouth, I pulled out my phone and typed "duck" into Google Maps. The first result was a craft beer spot in Koreatown that specialized in duck and deep-fried Oreos. And to complete the trifecta, it was dog-friendly.

Driving to the restaurant, I thought about my feelings. I thought about how I was going to be eating them soon. As a birder, craving duck while viewing one of the prettiest species of the family is a convoluted and guilt-ridden experience. Here was this animal that I admired—that I had pored over in books—and it also happened to be mouthwateringly delicious. It was a conundrum.

I got to the restaurant, snagged a table, and ordered a duck French dip sandwich and some fries cooked in duck fat. There was a dish on the menu called "Death by Duck," but I couldn't bring myself to order it. The image of a pair of mergansers sitting down to eat me for lunch came to mind.

The waiter brought over a bowl of water for Mochi and Bailey, who were hanging out under the table.

It really had turned out to be a great day after all. And I could see how the rest of the afternoon was going to unfold: I would stuff myself with food. Then I was going to need a nap.

The food arrived, and I sank into duck bliss.

Once I had regained my senses, I noticed that the pups were peering out from under the edge of the table, watching me eat. I was feeling generous—so I handed Mochi my hat. She politely took it and set it on the ground, rejecting my offer—and she and her brother continued to look up at me expectantly.

When it comes to my dogs, I'm a weak man. I slipped them each a piece of duck from my sandwich. Mochi gulped it down, and then put a paw on my knee, trying to pressure me into giving her more. Bailey practically inhaled the piece I gave him and then sat back down, licking the grease off his whiskers.

Mochi growled for more. She's always been pushier than her brother—she's cleverer than he is, too. They love to roughhouse together, and I once saw Mochi feign injury to trick him. Bailey had given her a nip on the leg, and she gave a strange yelp and pretended to limp away. When Bailey turned around, she pounced on him.

I told her to lie down and then gave her another piece of

duck. I gave one to Bailey, too. I didn't want him to think I was playing favorites.

The waiter came over, and I put in an order of deep-fried Oreos.

"You know, your one dog isn't looking so hot," he said.

I looked under the table. Mochi looked chipper enough, but Bailey was wheezing, his eyes closed. He took a long, rattling breath. He exhaled, and you could see he was struggling. I rubbed his back.

"What's going on, buddy?" I asked.

Bailey began to dry heave. Then he threw up.

The waiting room at the animal hospital was playing Christmas music. Obscure *animal-themed* Christmas music. I don't know how many of you know the song "Dominick the Donkey," but, trust me, it's not what you want to be listening to while you're waiting to find out if you poisoned your dog.

After what felt like an hour, the vet stepped into the waiting room and called me back to see Bailey. He was sitting on a stainless-steel table, looking like his normal self. He lifted his head and wagged his tail when he saw me.

"Bailey is going to be fine," the vet said. "He had a strong intolerance to something he ate—my guess would be the duck. If I were you, I'd consider getting him allergy tested. In the meantime, no more duck for Bailey."

In front of me, as I write this, I have a list of all the foods that Bailey can't eat per the allergy testing results. He is allergic to duck (of course), chicken, potatoes (both sweet and regular), eggs, fish (all kinds), wheat, venison, lamb, peanuts, soy, and chocolate (duh).

At my feet, Bailey is smiling up at me while his sister is gnawing at his ears. I've noticed that since I've changed his diet, he's stopped licking his paws as much, or scratching the top of his lip. Some hair has grown in around his nose that I didn't realize was missing. He used to paw at his face and get runny eyes, but no longer.

He's the healthiest dog I've ever met, and he now eats substantially better than I do: a blend of lean pork, quinoa, kale, Fuji apples, carrots, and various omega fatty acids not derived from fish.

Mochi eats dog food.

# HOW TO LOOK SEXY
## ON CAMERA

The first time Lucy and I ever kissed on-screen was in a bar in Vancouver. We were shooting the pilot, and there's a scene where we're making out in a bathroom.

I flossed at least three times before that scene. I had a bottle of mouthwash with me on set, and I gargled between every take. At dinner that night with the cast, everything tasted minty fresh, and the next day my mouth was numb.

The whole time I was shooting the pilot, I tried to keep in mind a piece of advice a model once gave me. She told me that if you ever want to look sexy on camera, you just have to pretend you're slightly confused about something. Not too confused, she said. You don't want to actually appear befuddled. Just a bit dazed.

That advice seemed to help, but there are a few other hurdles to looking sexy—and most of those hurdles for me involve hair.

I have a lot of stubble, no matter how often my face is shaved. The makeup team on *Pretty Little Liars* has to constantly reapply Lucy's makeup whenever we kiss because my cheeks always belt-sand it off.

Shaving has some consequences. Once, Lucy and I were filming a sex scene, and I had an ingrown hair on my neck from shaving. It was a big red bump—too big for makeup to completely hide. The DP tried different camera angles, but we were romping around in bed in the scene, so he couldn't get a bump-free view.

At one point, someone suggested putting a dab of green paint on it—the same color as a green screen—so that it could be edited out in post. Needless to say, having a crew of twenty-plus people obsessing over a blemish on my neck was a humbling experience.

Whenever I have a shirtless scene, I have to shave off all my chest hair. The network requires all the men on the show to have smooth, porpoise-y chests.

I tried waxing it once. Never again.

The week after I shave my chest, I'm always in agony. Itchy, itchy agony. I've tried everything to help cope with the pain: baby oil, coconut oil—even olive oil, but that just made me hungry. The only remedy that makes any difference whatsoever is Advil, two fingers of scotch, and patience.

If we're shooting a scene where I'm wearing a low-cut shirt or a Henley, Cindy from hair and makeup will use a vibrating mini razor called "the peanut"—I promise it's not a sex toy—and shave a deep "V" around the shirt line in my chest hair.

Strangely enough though, arm hair is always okay on *Pretty Little Liars*. That's how they want the guys to look: smooth in the middle, hairy at the edges. It's a strange formula.

So, I guess what I'm saying here is that, if you want to look sexy on camera, shave your chest and remember to look confused. Just not too confused.

# THE BIRDS

# AND THE BEES

My sister Sarah entered the world in San Diego, California. I was born three days and three years later a continent away, in Germany. Our parents were in the military, which is why we were stationed overseas. My mom was a nurse with the navy, and my dad was a journalist and editor at *Soldiers* magazine.

Sarah was two when they moved to Europe, so she remembers a lot more about Germany than I do. She's told me about the parks we used to go to, the bakeries and the shops near our home. I don't remember much of it. At the time I was primarily focused on crying and learning to walk.

On days when he didn't have work, my dad would take Sarah and me to the local *Tiergarten*—which translates, literally, to "animal garden." It was a zoo. I was too young to remember, but my dad says I was always drawn to the exotic birds. He says I used to run up and stick my fingers through the chain link of their cages to try to pet their wildly colored feathers. Perhaps the bird-loving die was cast before I even had a choice in the matter.

When I was three, my parents were called back stateside. We moved to Virginia, and my mom started working at a naval hospital in DC, and my dad started his next magazine gig. With both of my parents out of the house, my sister and I spent a lot of time with babysitters—I've mentioned before that I scared many of them off.

During this time, Sarah and I became inseparable. My mom used to joke that I was my big sister's shadow. Anywhere she went, I followed.

Sarah and I would play pretend for hours, lost in worlds of our own creation, and speaking languages nobody else could understand. Sarah would often set the rules of the world, and I would play the part she assigned to me.

We didn't have a dog, and we both really wanted one, so sometimes Sarah would have me run around on all fours and bark at cats. We had to stop that game though after I got carried away and chased a neighborhood boy back to his home.

A lot of our make-believe involved evil nuns. I'm not sure why. Maybe it had something to do with Sarah's love of everything British—and often stories involving British children would also feature a domineering lady of the cloth. Neither of us had ever seen a nun in real life, but we would spend hours pretending to fight them.

When one of us had to play a dreaded nun, Sarah always assigned the part to me.

At the time, my dad was reading Jane Goodall's books, and he would read to us from them. Goodall wrote extensively about chimpanzees and poaching in Africa, and we became obsessed with the settings of her stories. When we played outdoors, we would pretend that we were lost in tropical lands filled with wild tribes of cannibalistic nuns—all played by me.

When I was four, Virginia was hit by a terrible blizzard. Both of my parents stayed home from work for a week. That was the first time my mom and dad ever got to witness the full extent of our marathon make-believe sessions. During the storm, my dad helped Sarah and me turn a couch on its side. We covered it in sheets and created a fort in the living room. When my dad asked us what it was for, Sarah told him that we were defending our keep from a horde of Blessed Sisters.

My parents looked at each other, and my dad suggested, as diplomatically as possible, that perhaps we might want to try fighting something other than the Catholic Church. The idea had never occurred to us.

One day that spring, Sarah and I were spending the day at a babysitter's house, and we decided to run off into the backyard to play "Jane Goodall." We knew that there were poacher nuns everywhere—and rural Virginia was no exception.

In our search for poachers, we came across a large beehive in the trunk of a tree. Naturally, we whacked it with our nunchucks.

This turned out to be a terrible idea.

The hive exploded on the ground, unleashing a cloud of irate bees, hell-bent on revenge. As the first wave descended upon us, our babysitter grabbed her own baby—she was a mother—and ran inside, locking herself and her five-month-old in the bathroom.

Sarah and I ran into the house screaming after her and banged on the bathroom door, shouting to be let in.

"I'm so sorry," she cried from the other side of the door. "I can't. You'll let the bees in."

Just then, another bee stung me. On the eyelid. We had run inside without closing the back door.

The entire swarm had chased us into the house, and they weren't letting up. This was it. The bees had us exactly where they wanted us.

I asked Sarah if we were going to die.

"No!" she said. "I have an idea." Sarah was always coming up with clever solutions to impossible situations.

"Take your clothes off," she said, ripping off her shoes. "The bees won't recognize us if we're naked. They'll just keep attacking our clothes thinking it's us."

My God, she was brilliant. I immediately started taking off my pants. They got caught around my ankles, and I tripped on them and went down. Sarah pulled me up by my shoulders and helped me un-Velcro my shoes.

We hastily laid out our clothes on the floor like flattened scarecrows for the bees to find. What a great idea this was. Surely now, those dumb bees would stop stinging us and attack our clothes instead.

They didn't.

We ran around the babysitter's house naked, screaming, and crying as bees continued to sting us.

Mercifully, my dad came to pick us up early. As he walked

up the driveway, he was greeted by the sight of his two children, naked and screaming, pressed up against the bay windows. Our babysitter was still locked in the bathroom.

This might have been one of the only moments I can recall seeing my dad's military training in action. He took one look at us, ran to the front door, and kicked it in. I don't know if he even tried to turn the knob first.

He rushed to my sister and me, scooped us up in his arms, and sprinted to the car.

He took us home, gave us both oatmeal baths, and put antihistamine cream over all of our welts. We didn't go to the hospital, since my mom was a nurse, but I was still bedridden, waiting for the end to come.

I asked my father for a piece of paper.

"For what?" he asked.

"I want to write my will."

"Who are you going to give all your stuff to?"

"Sarah. For her bravery. And for saving my life."


When I was six, Sarah started taking voice lessons. She would come home every week with sheet music and new songs to learn. She'd lock herself in her room and practice scales for hours. It was the first time that my big sister had gone off to do something that I wasn't allowed to join.

I persuaded my parents to let me take voice lessons, too. I didn't really care about singing, but my sister was doing it, so I had to do it, too. I ended up developing a bit of a crush on my voice teacher, so I kept taking lessons as long as I could get my parents to let me.

Soon after I started taking voice lessons, Sarah and I started going to see local plays. Our aunt Jules worked at a nearby high school called Georgetown Prep—her first and only job: she's been there since 1970. Whenever they would put on a show, Sarah and I would get to see it.

Aunt Jules introduced us to the head of the school's drama department. We told him how much we liked his plays, and he asked us if we ever wanted to be a part of them. Often, the plays would have big ensemble scenes—villagers going about their days, workers in a factory, that kind of thing—and they didn't have enough actors to fill the stage. So my sister and I started acting in the big ensemble scenes of the shows.

Our first big scene was as tavern boys in the play 1776. We wiped down tables and carried around empty beer mugs in the background of the big musical numbers. We were in awe, completely starstruck by the teenage actors dancing and singing around us. Sarah's hair was short then, too, so we both played boys. It wasn't really a big deal for us—when we played pretend in the living room, Sarah and I switched genders constantly depending on the story we were telling.

The first time we acted in a play together, I almost backed out. Sarah calmed me down. She took my hand in hers and said, "It's okay, Ian. I'll be here. If you get scared just hug me and it'll be okay." She was right. Everything was okay. Everything was always okay when my big sister was nearby, and we ended up doing several plays together at the high school.

As is often the case with siblings, things changed when Sarah started middle school. I was still a little kid, but she was suddenly a teenager. She didn't want to play make-believe anymore.

We started to fight—all the time. For the first time in my

life, my sister and I didn't get along. Our status quo became conflict.

Once, when Sarah was babysitting me, I decided to hold her hostage and force her to be my friend again. I snuck up behind her while she was doing the dishes, and I pulled a butter knife on her.

"Freeze," I said, pointing the dull blade at her knees.

Sarah calmly reached into the dishwasher and pulled out a large kitchen knife. I burst into tears and ran to my room.

Over the next few years, Sarah and I grew more and more distant. Sarah was busy with her friends and her writing. I was busy losing the Geography Bee to Danny fucking Gordon.

I moved from elementary school to middle school. Sarah moved up to high school. All along, we were still bickering. By the time I started high school, we were barely on speaking terms.

I was going through adolescence. My body started to grow into my voice. I began going on dates. At school we learned sex ed—awkwardly enough, my sex-ed teacher was my aunt Jules.

In the winter of my freshman year of high school, Sarah asked me if we could go somewhere to talk.

There weren't a lot of restaurants or coffee shops near us when we were growing up. In fact, if you lived in Herndon and you needed to have a heart-to-heart with somebody, there was really only one place you could go. So we headed down to the Dairy Queen on Lynn Street.

Sitting across from Sarah on the red plastic bench in the

Dairy Queen, I found myself unable to maintain eye contact. It was cold outside, but I'd ordered a Blizzard—out of habit, I guess, or defiance. I was pretending to be interested in my ice cream so that I didn't have to look at my sister. I kept turning the cup upside down to see if anything would fall out of it.

Sarah spoke first.

"So, you like mint with Oreos?" she asked.

I was quiet. At first I acted like I hadn't heard her.

"Yeah, I always have," I finally said.

"You're right. I remember you, uh . . . yeah, you love mint."

Our conversation, if you could even call it that, had stalled. Again.

"You doing okay, though?"

I nodded. "Yeah, I'm fine."

She sighed, and covered her eyes with her hands.

"Look, the reason I wanted to talk to you is . . ."

She trailed off. The door swung open and a gorgeous woman in running clothes walked in. She passed by our table and I, being a fifteen-year-old boy, checked her out. I followed her to the counter with my eyes, then caught myself, felt guilty, and turned back to Sarah.

Sarah's eyes were locked on the woman, too. She might have been checking her out even harder than I was. After a moment, she laughed at herself, and turned back to me.

I could practically hear the lightbulb click on in my head.

"That's what I wanted to talk to you about. I'm a lesbian, Ian."

My mouth fell open. I didn't say anything. I didn't look away either.

Sarah and I sat like that for about a minute, just looking at one another in silence.

"I'm going to tell Mom and Dad tomorrow, and I just wanted to come out to you first. It's not a big deal. Just, you know, say something, yeah?"

I sat there for a moment, thinking about what I could possibly say to her.

Then it dawned on me. Sarah had just told me something that she must have been holding on to for years. It couldn't have been easy to share that with me, her bratty little brother, sitting on this cold bench in this small-town Dairy Queen. My sister was incredibly brave. Braver than anyone else I knew in my life at the time.

And I had something of my own that I'd been too proud—or too scared—to admit. When I opened my mouth, it was the only thing my body would let me say.

"I've really missed you, Sarah," I said, trying not to cry. "Thanks for letting me know."

Sarah smiled, and she settled back in her seat. We finished our ice cream, checked out the sexy jogger together one last time, then drove home.

# FIFTY SHADES OF

# THANKSGIVING

It was Wednesday afternoon. I stood in my backyard, hovering over a raw turkey. This was, in fact, a practice turkey. The next day, my dad, stepmom Mari, sister Sarah, and stepsister Erika would be coming over to spend Thanksgiving with me. Sarah lives in LA, but the rest had traveled across the country for the holiday.

I needed tomorrow's turkey to be perfect. I'd never hosted family before, and this was a chance for me to prove to them just how grown-up and competent I'd become since college. I'd thoroughly cleaned the house, even scrubbing the grout between the tiles in the shower. I wanted to make sure nothing was vulnerable to judgment.

The only obstacle that remained was the bird.

I'd never cooked a Thanksgiving turkey before. Or a non-Thanksgiving turkey, for that matter. I'm not exactly an expert in the kitchen. I was on an episode of my castmate Shay's YouTube cooking show once, and I accidentally brought cucumbers instead of zucchinis for the dish.

Shay, who happens to be Canadian, had a lot of advice about this traditional American meal. She said I should make a smoked turkey—that it would seal in the juices better than roasting it in the oven, and that I could ignore the turkey for a few hours while it smoked so I could tend to the rest of the meal.

I spent a few days looking up recipes online, falling deeper and deeper into a wormhole of culinary message boards. All the information on smoking turkeys was overwhelming, and often conflicting—so I kept reading.

There were websites where commenters made sweeping generalizations about how their way to smoke a turkey was the "right" way, going after anyone who disagreed. One guy got mocked because he only brined his turkey for ten hours. Another guy told him that if he didn't want to listen to Alton Brown, who advocated for a two-day brine, he was a fool. Self-proclaimed experts were throwing around advice for week-long brines and five-day thaws in the fridge. It got to the point where, to have a bird ready by late November, you needed to start planning in April.

I was intimidated—but I was also intrigued. After cross-referencing a number of recipes and YouTube videos, I finally decided on a foolproof plan.

It was time to find out if all that research was going to pay off. I checked the temperature on the grill to see if it was ready to put the bird on. It was nearly there.

When I first moved into my house on the east side of town, Sophia's dad gave me a Big Green Egg as a housewarming gift. The Big Green Egg is the Rolls-Royce of grill-smoker combos. It's substantially fancier than any grill ever needs to be—and it sent an unspoken message to all my friends that I was a substantially better chef than I actually am.

There's a community of Big Green Egg fanatics. They call themselves "Eggheads," and every year they gather in the Midwest for something called "Eggtoberfest." Owning one of the grills put me on the mailing list, but I've yet to attend one of their big annual events.

Smoke was beginning to pour out of the top of the grill. I'd set hickory blocks on top of lump charcoal, and it smelled delicious. I checked the thermometer again—it was hot enough to put the bird on.

I opened up the Big Green Egg and placed the turkey on the grill and quickly realized: my Big Green Egg was not big enough. Perhaps I had a medium Green Egg, or an egg-sized Green Egg. Either way, the lid wasn't about to fit over the turkey. It couldn't. The legs and wings of the bird jutted out over the edges.

I looked down at the turkey—plump from the two-day brine—that I'd trussed up earlier in the kitchen. It was sprawled helplessly on the grill, waiting patiently to be smoked. It looked oddly sexual, with twine wrapped around various body parts. I had auditioned for the lead role in *Fifty Shades of Grey* a couple of months before, and this turkey was giving me flashbacks.

I could cook this bird, I thought, but it wasn't going to be pretty.

I got some more twine and used it to tie the top of the grill down as best I could.

I picked up a couple of bricks off the ground and balanced them on the lid of the grill for added weight. It wasn't fully closed, and it didn't look even remotely safe, but some smoke was getting trapped in the grill now, and it looked like the bird had a chance at cooking.

I cast one last worried look at the precariously balanced turkey and my makeshift grilling solution, and I went inside.

The recipe called for the turkey to be rebasted every hour for three hours. I had time to get cleaned up and answer a few emails. I hopped into the shower.

A few minutes later, I heard a loud crash outside. I put on a towel and ran upstairs.

The bricks had fallen off the Big Green Egg. The top had flown open, and the turkey had rolled off the grill and onto the ground. It was now caked in dirt with a few burn marks scattered across its skin.

Mochi and Bailey rushed over, assuming that this must be their supper. They wagged their thanks to the dog gods and tried to dig in.

I shooed them away and inspected the bird to see if any parts of it were salvageable. None were.

I hauled the turkey back inside and threw it away. I needed a solution, and I needed it by tomorrow morning. The grill definitely wasn't going to work.

I decided to just cook the turkey in the oven. It wouldn't be unusual, it wouldn't be unlike anything my family had ever tasted, but, with any luck, it also wouldn't be a total disaster.

The next morning, most of the fam arrived just before noon: my dad, Mari, and Erika. Sarah was coming a bit later.

My dad is a military historian. He has never not had a beard—I'm convinced that he was born with a goatee. My step-mom Mari is fluent in several languages, knows more about wine than the grapes themselves, and is one of the most supportive, upbeat people I have ever known.

Divorces are hard. They can rip families apart at the seams. But there can be a couple of positives. If you're lucky—and I was—you can end up with some totally badass stepsiblings. That's where Erika comes in. Erika lives on a farm in Northern California, before which she was interning on a small ten-acre veggie operation outside of Portland, Oregon. I went out to help her a couple years ago and was humbled. What gym-carved muscles I had were no match for actual labor, and before we broke for lunch, I had to lie down in a field of shallots and hold my hand over my mouth so the other farm hands couldn't hear me whimpering. Farmers are the strongest people I've ever met.

I helped my dad carry the luggage into the house and showed everyone to their rooms. While they were unpacking, I went upstairs to check on the turkey. I was slow-cooking it—at an extremely low temperature—so it had been in the oven since five in the morning.

I checked the meat thermometer. Everything seemed to be on track. This turkey was going to be delicious. The meal would be a hit. My family was going to be blown away.

I set the oven timer and went to go see if anyone needed any other grown-up items: a newspaper, extra towels, cufflinks, that sort of thing.

Once everyone was settled in, we gathered in the living room to catch up. There's a tradition in my family: pregaming. We've been pregaming Thanksgiving ever since I can remember.

Around 2:00 P.M., various Thanksgiving-themed finger foods are set out on the kitchen island, along with at least three bottles of wine.

A lot had changed since I'd last seen my family. My dad was working on a new book, Mari's wine-importing business was expanding, and Erika had just settled into the new farm in Northern California. All my dad wanted to talk about, though, was *Pretty Little Liars*.

My dad and Mari hold viewing parties at their home in Virginia. Every time a new episode comes out, they gather a dozen or so of their close friends to have dinner and watch the show. I always smile when I think about it. I have this image of a room full of middle-aged professionals—doctors, lawyers, military historians—all dressed to the nines, gathered around my dad's living room TV, watching season after season of this teen drama.

When I was growing up, my dad didn't watch much television. He had a little set, but it was nothing fancy. Then I landed a job on *PLL*, and he upgraded to a state-of-the-art flat screen with surround sound.

They've been hosting their viewing parties since the show started. By now, my dad and Mari's friends know more about the show than I do. They are current on all of the gossip, all of the rumors and fan theories, all of the Easter eggs that the show has to offer.

Recently, I went home for a long weekend, and one of my dad's friends—a 60-year-old periodontist named Phil—cornered me after dinner and told me he'd done the math and he'd figured out who "A" was.

"It's Aria, isn't it?" he said, examining my reactions closely. "You can tell me."

I told him, honestly, "I have no idea who 'A' is."

He frowned, looked me over, then smiled as if he'd worked something out in his head. "I hear you," he said. "NDAs, right?" He winked. "Don't worry. I won't tell." He laughed and strolled back to the table to help my dad put the dishes away.

The smell of turkey was beginning to fill the house.

On the couch, Mari and my dad were laughing. "Should we tell him?" she asked.

My dad shook his head. "He'll be too embarrassed."

"He won't be embarrassed," she said, still giggling. "He'll think it's funny," She leaned forward to get my attention: "Ian, we saw the funniest article about you the other day. Do you read Perez Hilton?"

"No," I said. "Do *you*?"

My dad shrugged. "It's not that bad. Erika, did you bring your laptop?"

She had, and ran downstairs to get it. When I protested, Mari simply refilled my wine glass. Erika came back with the laptop, and we gathered around the sofa to have a look.

"It's really not bad at all, Ian," Mari said. "Steve, what was the title of the article?"

"It's . . . uh . . . wow, I can't remember."

"Here, let's just look up your name." She typed "Ian Harding" into Google and hit enter. On the top of the results page was a row of photographs of me smiling. "Look at all of these nice photos of you!" she said. She clicked an image, and it opened up a page of dozens of photos of me grinning on red carpets.

Erika laughed. "Why do you always look so squinty in these photos? Are the lights really bright, or are you just trying to look sexy?"

My dad chimed in: "I think it has to do with animal instinct. When we squint as humans, we're signaling to a possible mate that—"

"I do it because one eye is bigger than the other," I said, cutting off his evolutionary theory.

All three members of the family crowded up close to my face.

"No you don't!"

"It's not really—well . . ."

"Oh yeah, I guess you do!"

Self-consciously, I turned back to the screen and started scrolling.

And that's when we saw them.

Down at the bottom of the second page, clustered on the right side of the screen, were a handful of terribly Photoshopped images of me completely naked, always with a comically large erection.

"Is that . . . ?" Mari said.

"No!" I shouted. "No, of course not. That's not me!"

The room was very quiet. My dad suddenly became interested in the bookshelves across the room and walked away. Erika stood slightly behind her mom, tears of silent laughter filling her eyes.

"Wait, Mari, do you think that's real?!" I asked.

"Well I didn't look at it long enough to take an educated guess!"

Erika lost it and burst out laughing. I assured Mari that I would only ever do full-frontal for HBO, then excused myself to go check on the turkey.

Erika joined me in the kitchen, still laughing, and began to chop veggies for a salad.

As she and I cooked, I noticed Mari had sat back down at Erika's laptop.

I called over: "Are you still looking for that article? Seriously Mari, I believe you when you say it's funny, but you don't . . ."

I realized she wasn't looking at me as I spoke. Her eyes went wide and her mouth fell open. She stood and brought the computer over to where Erika and I were standing.

"I . . . I googled 'Ian Harding fan,' and this came up . . ."

I looked at the screen. I began reading what looked like an interview, but my costar Drew was also part of the interview.

It wasn't an interview.

"Wait, Mari, what is this?"

She pointed, finger trembling, to the middle of the page. I began to read out loud: "He pulled off his boxers instantly, revealing his bare ass. Jason sighed, stepping forward. He dropped his belt, jeans, and boxers as well, and then made Ezra bend over the couch—"

Mari yanked the laptop out of my hands and snapped it shut.

"You know what," she said, "I'm all for loving who you want to love and freedom of expression and all that jazz, but I have to say, I'm not really interested in reading this about my stepson!"

I turned to Erika, who a moment ago had stood by my side but was now crumpled on the floor, convulsing with laughter.

"Is she dead?" My sister Sarah stood at the top of the stairs. We hadn't heard her come in.

"We were just reading some of my erotic fan fiction," I said.

"The gay or the straight stuff?"

"The what now?"

"The gay or the straight stuff? The hetero fan fiction is super dull. You basically just make Lucy soup when she's sick or, like, fix her bike while wearing plaid. The gay stuff, on the other hand, that can get pretty interesting."

"Wait, you knew about this?"

She walked over to the kitchen island and popped a chip in her mouth. "Yup. One of my friends from back home found a few of them and emailed me. I can't believe you didn't know about them."

My dad had had enough of the bookshelves, and came back over to refill his wine glass.

"Are we done talking about my son the porn star?"

Right on cue, the oven timer went off. I donned a pair of oven mitts and took out the turkey—it was perfectly golden. It was time to eat.

The meal was a hit. We ate our faces off, piling on the stuffing and gravy and Brussels sprouts.

As Erika handed me a platter of sweet potatoes, I asked if anyone had gotten a chance to talk with Aren that day. Aren is Mari's son, Erika's brother, and he couldn't make it out to LA that Thanksgiving because of school.

"I did," Erika said. "He sends his love to everyone. He said he wishes he could be here, but he's got a lot on his plate right now."

My dad coughed, and indicated the plate overflowing with food in front of him.

"I've got a feeling he's going to love hearing about your fan fiction, though," Erika continued. "Maybe he can read a passage at the next *PLL* party our parents throw."

It seemed so natural when she said it that it didn't hit me until later in the conversation.

"Our parents."

The first few years after my mom and dad got divorced, the holidays were tense, almost bitter. Sarah and I were angry. Yet now, years later, I find myself looking forward to family gatherings—they are different than before, yes, but families change, and this one is mine now.

# THE CALIFORNIA
## CONDOR

The California condor once ranged from Canada to Mexico—and could be spotted as far away as the East Coast—but by the early 1980s, only twenty-two remained in the wild. Due to a massive conservation and reintroduction program, the population has since grown to just over two hundred birds, but they are still at risk of extinction.

Condors are massive. They can soar up to 15,000 feet above the ground and are often mistaken for small aircraft. With their ten-foot wingspan, they are by far the largest flying bird on the continent.

As humans, we have an interesting attachment to big, majestic birds. We like to tie big, lofty ideas to them. Take the bald eagle, for example. Really pretty and really big. It isn't just a bird for Americans. Bald eagles mean freedom. They mean liberty, justice, victory. Bald eagles have become a stand-in for all the values that our country holds dear. That's a lot of pressure to put onto one bird, no matter how big and majestic it may be. Which, in my opinion, is why the turkey would never have worked as our national bird. No offense to Benjamin Franklin, who preferred them over bald eagles, but turkeys just aren't regal enough to support that much symbolism.

Since we love attaching big ideas to big birds so much, I'm going to do the same with condors. Bear with me here, but I'm going to say that—for me, at least—the California condor is a metaphor for great, meaningful acting roles—the kinds of roles you see pop up once, maybe twice, in a lifetime.

Like outstanding roles, encountering a condor is rare, incredibly rewarding, and, often, a huge surprise. Nowadays, California condors only live in extremely remote, craggy, hard-to-get-to locales. So to see one—much like booking a dream role—you have to either put in a lot of hard work or be ridiculously lucky. Usually both.

Last summer, my friend Walter and I drove out to Pinnacles National Park to try to get a glimpse of one. Our friend John was supposed to come with us, but John—who, as I've mentioned before, only goes birding when forced to do so—had said that he would rather get run over by a car than go look at birds with me again.

And that's what he did. John called me the day before the trip to say that a car had hit him while he'd been riding his bicycle and he couldn't come on the trip.

I called bullshit. John had tried to sneak out of birding trips in the past. "Prove it," I said.

John hung up the phone.

Five seconds later, he FaceTimed me. I answered the call, and there was John, holding up his blood-soaked arms. "Enjoy your sky rats," he cackled into the screen. "Have fun without me."

"Go to a hospital, John," I said.

He shrugged and told me he was going to make breakfast first, then signed off.

Walter drove over to my house early that Saturday morning. We loaded my car with camping gear, quickly downed some coffee, and set off for Pinnacles.

Pinnacles is one of the newest national parks in the country. President Obama gave it its park status in 2013. It's a pretty cool spot, and out of the way, so not many people visit.

I had been looking forward to the trip for weeks, but that morning I was particularly happy to be going. I'd had an audition for a lead role in a Netflix show earlier that week, and I'd felt really good about it, but my manager had called me late Friday night to let me know that I hadn't gotten it. I don't tend to get worked up about auditions—rejection is a huge part of being an actor, and I usually don't let it get to me—but I was glad to have an excuse to get out of LA for a couple days just the same.

After driving all morning, we made it to the park. We noticed driving in that the ranger station had its own swimming pool. We thought about taking a dip, but we hadn't come to swim. We drove farther down the road to look for a campsite instead. We needed to get hiking soon if we were going to have any chance of spotting a condor.

The park was pretty empty that weekend, so we had our pick of campsites. We ended up finding a beautiful little spot nestled in the shade of two big oak trees and just a few steps away from a small, gurgling creek.

The first thing we noticed as we pulled up to the campsite was that there were California quail everywhere. Seriously, everywhere. Not flocks, either—they moved in herds. Whole sections of ground were covered, absolutely blanketed in sheets of quail.

We left our tents and bags in the car for the time being and drove over to one of the major trailheads. Condors nest in caves high up in the cliffs, so we had to get some altitude to get a chance to see them. We decided to start out on the Moses Spring Trail—a nice warm-up hike before the vertical trek up the mountainside.

Hiking up the mountain, we crossed through several distinct habitat zones. Occasionally the elevation change can make for some pretty interesting overlap. Normally scrub jays prefer—as their name would suggest—lowland scrub, whereas Steller's jays like a bit more altitude and forest. But, at one point hiking up, we saw both perched side by side.

It was a great day for birds. We saw a big flock of American goldfinches, a few California towhees, a Nuttall's woodpecker, and a black-throated gray warbler—probably getting ready to begin its migration back south for the winter. Off in the distance, we heard a canyon wren, its lonesome descending call echoing across the rock faces, like a cartoon character falling off a cliff.

These were all excellent birds, but they weren't the one I was here for.

None of them were condors.

The trail led us past a small group of rock climbers resting on their crash mats and up to the mouth of a cave. A sign in front of the cave advised us that flashlights were required for entry. I turned on my headlamp and stepped inside.

These caves were not what you might ordinarily think of when you hear the word "cave." There were no stalactites or stalagmites, no glowing insects or crazy deformed cave slugs. The tunnels were created by a series of boulders that were rolled up on top of one another. It looked like the aftermath of a snowball fight between giants, and walking through the caves felt like exploring the underbelly of a rockslide. Light broke through the stones at odd angles and zigzagged its way down to us in faint bursts, giving hints of color to the moss that covered the ground at our feet. It was cooler in here as well.

The rangers were right to put up that flashlight sign. At times, the boulders clustered together pretty tightly, and Walter and I were plunged into total darkness. The path in front of us got narrower and narrower as it got harder to see. I tightened the strap on my headlamp and looked back to make sure Walter was doing all right. He was about ten paces behind me, his flashlight still packed away in his bag.

"Aren't you going to turn your light on?" I asked.

He laughed. "I can see just fine without it."

Moments later, I heard a thud behind me. "Ow," Walter muttered, and then he turned his light on.

The caves sloped up, and suddenly the tunnel was flooded with light. As we stepped out, we realized that we were now on top of the boulder field. We jogged up a couple of flights of stone steps and found ourselves looking out over a reservoir. A thin grove of trees lined the edge of the water at intervals on

the far shore. A snake swam lazily across the water's surface, its black-and-yellow-striped body glistening in the midday sun.

The reservoir was pretty small: Walter pointed out that it was roughly the size of an Olympic pool.

The Olympics were going on in Rio that week. It was all over the news. And for some reason, hearing the word "Olympic"—thinking about sports, about competition and medals—got me thinking about the audition I'd just had again.

Most Olympic sports have clear winners. The criteria for success in a foot race is purely objective. There are no extra points for style, haircut, or music choice. You are the best if and only if you have the best time or the most points. It's simple. There's something comforting about that kind of objectivity.

Acting is the exact opposite. It is purely subjective. Despite the awards given out every year, there are no clear and universally accepted ways to determine what makes one actor better than another. You go into an audition, and you worry about being a good actor, about portraying the role as honestly and compellingly as possible. But you worry about your acting because it is the only thing you have any control over.

A host of other factors can determine whether or not you get the role, and there's nothing you can do about them. Casting often depends on your social media following, on what producers you know, whether or not your previous films made money, whether or not you've been in the news lately, what kind of relationship your agents have with the casting office. And so on.

Just after college I met a casting director at a house party in LA. After we'd introduced ourselves, I asked him to tell me about his job. I wanted to know how hard it was to figure out who the best actor in the room was.

He laughed. "If all I had to do was say who the best actor in the room was, anybody could do my job," he said. "Also, I'd get to go home a hell of a lot earlier at night."

Maybe that's what we like so much about Olympic sports: when there are objective winners and losers, life feels a whole lot simpler and fairer. We can argue until we're blue in the face about whether or not Meryl Streep is the greatest living actor, citing opinions and personal preference, but the whole world agrees that Usain Bolt is the greatest living sprinter because, well, math. It's a rare and fascinating experience to have the entire world agree about something. How often do you get to see that?

Walter tapped me on my shoulder and broke me out of my daydreaming. "What's that over there?" he asked, pointing at a speck in the sky.

I looked up. It was definitely a bird. And it was big. Really big. Possibly even condor big. Reminding myself not to get too excited, I clutched my binoculars and lifted them to my face to get a closer look.

It was a golden eagle.

Son of a bitch.

Don't get me wrong, this was a pretty cool thing to see. It was, in fact, my first time ever seeing a golden eagle. By all accounts, I should have been dancing with joy.

But it wasn't a condor, and so I saved my dancing for later. It's bizarre seeing a bird you've always wanted to see and feeling disappointed by it. I felt bird-spoiled. Like the kid who gets a car for their sixteenth birthday but gets mad because it isn't an Audi.

Seeing the eagle meant that we were high enough up the mountain to start looking for condors, so we scanned the horizon with our binoculars as we walked along the water's edge. We had to be careful not to get tricked by any turkey vultures. Turkey vultures often get mistaken for condors, and condors often get mistaken for small planes. We saw both turkey vultures and small planes flying over the reservoir that afternoon, but no condors.

After a few minutes of scanning the sky to no avail, we heard footsteps on the trail behind us. We put our binoculars down and turned to see a couple in their thirties coming up the path. From the way they waved and greeted us it seemed like they wanted to stop and chat for a bit.

Walter and I introduced ourselves. It turned out the couple was visiting from Germany—the woman was in town for a scientific entrepreneurship conference, and her husband was tagging along for fun. He had a camera with him, and he was taking pictures of everything. He showed us some of his favorites from the day: pretty leaves, oddly shaped rocks, the sweaty T-shirt of a man they'd passed on the trail. He was a photo nut.

"You know, if you're looking for cool things to photograph, we just saw a snake swimming in the reservoir over there," I said, pointing to where we'd seen it a few minutes before.

The man let out an excited yip, grabbed his camera bag, and set off jogging toward the water. His wife looked down and noticed that Walter and I were wearing binoculars.

"Oh!" she said. "Are you two here to see the condor?"

We nodded.

"Have you seen it?" she asked.

"No, no luck yet," I said. "We were thinking we might have to hike up to the top to get a look at them."

She smiled and wished us luck. Apparently they had come to the park with the same goal. As we spoke, her husband came back, a little winded but happy. He'd gotten a good shot of the snake, he said.

Walter and I resumed our hike. As we said goodbye, the German couple was sitting down on a boulder so that the husband could show his wife his snake photos.

We left the Moses Spring Trail and got onto the High Peaks Trail, which would take us up to the summit. The sky was cloudless that day, just a wash of blue with blinding sunlight in the west. We hiked along, spotting birds as we went.

Birding up in the mountains, especially on a day like that, can be difficult. You're staring intently at a tiny black spot set against a sea of blue, and your eyes keep going out of focus, because, naturally, they want to avoid staring directly up at the sun for too long. It's tough to differentiate any clear markings when it's that sunny out and everything you're looking at is hundreds of yards away. If you're not careful, hope and blurred vision can mess with your head—you become convinced that a tiny black dot in the sky is something special, even though you have absolutely no evidence to support it.

The trail sloped upward and broke into a series of switchbacks, cutting its way up the mountainside. As we trudged our way along the second switchback, a merlin flew over our heads. A merlin—aside from being the name of a badass wizard who aged in reverse—is a neat little falcon. Back in medieval times, merlins were the official bird of choice for noblewomen. They called them "lady hawks," and they used them to hunt skylarks.

The switchbacks were getting steeper and steeper. We decided to take a quick break and rehydrate a little. As Walter and I shuffled along looking for a nice spot to sit, we spotted the German couple again—and they were in front of us? When we'd left them, they'd been sitting on a boulder, looking at pictures, and somehow they'd beaten us up the mountain to where we now saw them, also sitting on a boulder and looking at pictures.

They were like lazy teleporters.

When they saw us, they both waved enthusiastically and beckoned us over.

"How—how did you get in front of us?" I asked, still panting from the trek up.

My question seemed to be lost in translation. The wife smiled and shrugged. "Ja, you know," she said, then nudged her husband. "Show them the photo. We saw the condor!"

We were shocked. "Here?" Walter asked. I looked up at the sky. Nothing. Just blue as far as the eye could see.

"Ja," the husband said, cycling through the photos on his screen to find the picture.

"Are you sure?" I asked.

"White on the wings, ja?" he said, his nose still buried in his camera.

Walter couldn't believe it. "Yeah!" he said. "Yeah, white on the wings."

The California condor has an unmistakable strip of pure white shooting across the underside of each of its wings.

"Aha!" the husband cried, finding the photo and handing the camera to us.

On the screen was a perfectly clear, crisp, beautifully captured photo of a turkey vulture.

"See the white?" he said, pointing at the tips of the vulture's wings. They were indeed pale—a light, silvery gray that verged on white—but nothing like the shocking white strip on a condor's wings.

This was awkward. Walter gave me a look. We had a heartbreaking decision to make. Did we tell him the truth, or did we let him go home, thinking he'd seen a condor when in fact he hadn't? Maybe a friend from home would tell him the truth about the bird. Maybe not; maybe he'd never find out. Maybe he'd always believe that he'd seen a condor. He'd go to his grave with that beautiful, happy lie.

I've heard birding described as the last bastion of honesty. We don't have big competitions, rivalries, or races. There is no world's greatest birder. There's no way for us to measure or rate success like you do in sports. If somebody says they've seen a bird, there's no real way to confirm or deny that they saw what they say they did unless they took a picture. The birding community as a whole depends on message boards run by enthusiasts from every corner of the earth. The honor code is all we have.

Most of the time, when you're out birding, it's just you and yourself, and if you can't be honest with yourself, what's the point? Birding cannot exist without honesty.

We decided to tell the Germans that they hadn't actually seen a condor, that it had just been a turkey vulture.

They were crestfallen. We felt terrible. The wife whispered

to me, "Ah, you shouldn't have told us." Meanwhile, the husband began to scroll through his camera, showing us all the photos he had taken of the vulture, trying to prove to us that it had, in fact, been a condor.

We felt bad and decided to get out of there. Walter led the way as we resumed hiking up the switchbacks, and we were quickly out of sight of the Germans.

As we hiked on, I kept glancing up at the sky. Turkey vultures circled overheard, but definitely no condors up there. Not yet, at least. Walter was looking up, too. "I wish we could find some rangers," he said. "They could probably tell us where to look."

As he spoke, we rounded a corner and found ourselves face-to-face with a park ranger. Walter practically ran into him. I think we may have seemed a bit too excited.

"You guys okay?" he said.

"Totally. We're hoping to get a look at some of the condors today. Has anyone reported any sightings of them today?"

He shook his head. "Not my area, guys. You'd have to ask Condor Crew."

"Condor Crew?" Walter asked.

"Yeah," he said, offering no other explanation. "They'd be the ones to ask." Apparently this ranger was not going to be the solution to all of our condor problems.

We walked on. I never did find out what Condor Crew was.

Eventually, the switchbacks ended and we found ourselves on top of the mountain, surrounded by the pinnacles themselves. Pinnacles National Park is named for the sharp, pointy crags that line the top of its tallest mountain, jutting out at all angles like a mouth full of rotten teeth. Despite that description, they are a gorgeous sight, and there are no trees at that altitude, so standing among them you can see for miles in every direction.

We scrambled across the pinnacles and found a nice spot to perch and look out with our binoculars. There were vultures everywhere. I kept thinking each and every one of them was a condor. I can see how the German couple had made that mistake. The two different species look so similar at a distance—they were all just specks in the sky. I kept feeling a small jolt of excitement at each new little black dot, but none of them were what I hoped they would be.

California condors weren't always such a rarity in this part of the country. Hundreds of them once filled the sky. The land surrounding pinnacles is mostly agricultural, so pesticides took out a big percentage of the condor population, but that wasn't the only factor in their decline.

Johnny Cash helped too.

He had a ranch up in Ventura County, and he used to throw sloppy, debaucherous parties up there. Then in the mid-1960s, Cash got really into party buses. He would drive them out onto his property, hook up rows and rows of speakers, and blare out Christmas music as loud as he could into the mountains around him. But then one time his party bus overheated, and he set fire to the entire Las Casitas National Forest. The fire spread across three mountains, and hundreds of acres went up in flame.

At the time of the fire, the area was home to fifty-three California condors. Supposedly, Johnny Cash killed forty-nine of them.

When asked about the fire, he was decidedly unapologetic,

telling a judge, "I don't care about you or your damn yellow buzzards."

I don't think Johnny Cash and I would have liked each other.

Up in the sky, a single bird was flying off toward the horizon. It was just a speck, but it was a massive speck—much bigger than the buzzards circling nearby. I pulled out my binoculars. In the lenses, I could make out its wide black wings. But I couldn't see anything else. It was too far away.

I asked Walter, "Do you think that was it?"

He shrugged. He'd seen the bird, too, but neither of us could get a good enough look to ID it. If it was a turkey vulture, it was the biggest turkey vulture I'd ever seen. But I couldn't be positive that it wasn't.

I was defiant. It must have been a condor. What else could it have been?

I sat down and took out my bird journal. When I first started birding, I hated the idea of keeping a "life list." It felt like I was collecting birds. I thought that keeping track of them—writing down what I'd seen and where—would somehow cheapen the experience. I worried that I was making my hobby competitive. I had this image in my head of two birders comparing life lists, and one of them walking away as the "winner."

I've since come around to the practice, though. A life list is my own personal diary of what I've seen—and it wouldn't be worth anything to anyone else. Also, I have a terrible memory, so I need it.

I opened the book to the first available page and wrote down the date. After the date, I wrote "California condor" and then, to the right of that . . .

I couldn't do it. I couldn't say for certain that I'd actually seen it. I would never really know for sure, and it wasn't something I was willing to lie about. The honor code really sucks sometimes.

I scribbled "Better view needed" into the margin next to the condor's name and closed my book.

Walter squinted at the sun. It was lower now. It would be dark in a couple of hours, and we still needed to set our tents up down below.

As we began our descent, we saw the German couple appear again just over the ridge of the pinnacles. I considered waving goodbye, but they hadn't seen us yet, and I was worried they might still be upset about the turkey vulture. I didn't want to rub salt in the wound. I hope that the Germans had better luck with the condors than we did.

We walked down flights of steps that had been jackhammered into the mountainside by some brave construction crew. The trail home was faster—going downhill usually is. We passed a rock on our right that was absolutely covered in turkey vultures. They eyed us interestedly as we walked by—waiting to eat us in case we didn't make it down the mountain.

"Good ol' Mount Turkey Vulture," Walter said. I scowled. Up by the pinnacles, so many vultures had disappointed me when I'd mistaken them for condors. There was a smug, almost mocking, look on their bald, ugly faces.

If I can stick with the metaphor of condors being a stand-in for big acting roles, then turkey vultures are like auditions. Every time you see one, you think, "Oh my God, this could be it. This could be the big one."

But more often than not what you're seeing isn't a condor at all. It's just a big ol' turkey vulture.

We hiked on in silence for about half an hour. From time to time, a sparrow or a towhee would fly by us, but we weren't really paying much attention to the little stuff at that point. We were tired and hungry, and dinner and sleep were calling.

Near the end of the hike, I heard a light rustling of wings. An American kestrel came cruising along the side of the slope we were walking along. It landed in a tree a short distance in front of us.

I wouldn't say I have a favorite bird, but kestrels are definitely up there. They're hands-down the coolest.

American kestrels are small falcons—and no joke, they're red, white, and blue in color. I've seen one hover in place for minutes on end, then cartwheel through the air to nab some unwitting insect.

Kestrels—and falcons in general—are more closely related to parrots than to other kinds of hawks. I like to imagine they're little carnivorous parrots, though maybe that's not quite biologically correct.

Seeing the kestrel cheered me up. My feet were feeling lighter as we arrived at the end of the trail and began our short drive back to the campsite.

Heading back felt like driving through the opening scene of *Bambi*. There were quail all over the road. We passed mama deer with their fawns trailing behind them. Flocks of turkeys bobbed about in the bushes.

When we got back to the campsite and started setting up our tents, a cheeky raccoon came right up to beg for food. I turned to Walter: "We're trapped in a Disney movie."

It felt good being back at camp, surrounded by animals, feeling like a welcome guest in a wild habitat. I started thinking about my audition again, and about the condor. My mind wandered.

I think the thing about birding—about loving the outdoors in general—is that to do it, you need to find something in nature that is just yours, something that nobody else can touch or take away from you. It isn't about one specific bird. You can't be a birder who only wants to see one bird. That's not birding; that's an obsession. When you become a birder, you do it as a life plan.

Acting's the same. You have to find something you love about it that doesn't depend on anybody else. It isn't about booking one specific role on one specific day. If you just keep concentrating on the things you're not seeing, if you keep focusing on not getting the role, you're kind of missing the point. Nobody has ever seen every single bird on the planet. It would be impossible. No actor has booked every single role—the world would just be one giant monologue.

We had set out that morning to see the California condor. We hadn't seen it, and I'd felt grumpy all day as a result. But I'd seen half a dozen birds that I had never seen before. It was a day of discovery for me. The only choice I had was whether or not I embraced that discovery.

There would be other birds, other days spent outside, other chances to see the skies filled with flying colors. One bad day doesn't magically make you stop being a birder. One bad audition doesn't mean you aren't an actor anymore.

For dinner, we made pasta on a gas camping stove. We hadn't seen any condors, but it had been an undeniably good day for birds. I popped open a bottle of Apothic Red—my mom's favorite wine—and poured it into our metal camping mugs.

I turned to Walter and held up my mug. "To the American kestrel," I said.

"To the turkey vulture," he replied.

After we ate, we sat outside our tents looking at stars. Walter asked me if I knew any of the constellations.

"I know Orion, but that's about it."

"I actually know the bird ones," he said.

I didn't know there were any bird constellations.

He pointed at a big star above us, and I followed him as he traced a cross in the sky with his finger, connecting the first star to half a dozen others. "Cygnus," he said. "The Swan."

"It looks more like a cross," I said.

"Yeah, it's also called the Northern Cross. The Greeks knew it as Cygnus."

Walter pointed up to another star.

"See that one?" he asked.

I squinted. I could just make out a dim star where his finger was pointing.

"Follow it down and to the left," he said. "See it? Now from there, go to the right and a little down."

I got lost. Walter had to trace it out two more times before I could see what he was pointing at: Aquila, Zeus's eagle.

"Aquila carried Zeus's thunderbolts for him when he fought the Titans," he said. "At the end of his life, Zeus placed Aquila among the stars to thank him for his service."

Constellations always seem to overwhelm me with emotions. Looking up at the stars that night, I felt the usual cliché: I was a small and insignificant cog in the larger workings of the vast and limitless cosmos, and it was a humbling experience.

But I also felt the cliché's exact opposite. I realized that I was sitting there staring up at the exact same stars that people had stared at, named, and personified thousands of years before I was ever born. Before my country ever existed. Before my language was first spoken. These stories and these names had come down through an endless stream of shared narratives, shared values, beliefs, and stories. And they had arrived here. At the dawn of the twenty-first century, I was listening to tales and learning names from the beginning of humanity. The name Aquila had not faded with time. Nor had Cygnus. The names had outlived their creators by millennia.

I didn't make it into my tent that night. I fell asleep under the stars. Shortly before dawn, I woke up shivering and crawled into the tent, wrapping myself up like a burrito in my sleeping bag.

I tried to go back to sleep, but I was wide awake.

I pulled my sleeping bag around my shoulders and stepped out of the tent. The sun was poking out from behind the mountains to the east. I sat on a stump and watched it rise. Within half an hour, the campsite was flooded with radiant pink and orange tones.

I walked out into the street to get a better view of the sunrise. As I did, I heard the distant patter of small feet—dozens of them—running along the road. It sounded like a stampede of pygmy buffalo was coming up behind me.

A herd of quail rounded a corner and hustled toward me. They moved as one, curving this way and that like a rushing stream as they overtook the road. Despite their minute size, I

was genuinely frightened. A headline flashed in my head:
ACTOR TRAMPLED TO DEATH BY QUAIL AT SUNRISE VISTA.

I didn't know where I could run to avoid them, so I stood
my ground.

The quail rushed forward, their tiny feet pounding against
the asphalt in a muffled din. I closed my eyes as the first quail
reached my feet. This was it. Time to get pecked to death.

I felt something soft brush against my right ankle. Then
against my left. I felt wind and fluff and dust breezing lightly
by my calves. I opened my eyes.

The herd had not stopped, nor even slowed. The quail continued to rocket down the street, but they had parted at my
feet like water around a stone, doing their best to avoid this
unexpected human obstruction in their path. It was incredible. I felt like the Moses of fowl. Or perhaps I was a quail
whisperer.

When the quail had passed, I walked back to camp and sat
on a tree stump. I waited for Walter to get up.

When he appeared, we agreed to grab breakfast on the road
instead of cooking up something at the campsite. He had a lunch
date, and I needed to get back to LA for a fund-raiser that night.
We loaded up the car and hit the road.

On the way out of the park, we stopped at the ranger station to use their bathrooms. As we were getting back in our
car, a golf cart pulled into the parking lot near us. The park
ranger behind the wheel waved good morning.

"Just getting in or heading out?" he asked.

"Heading out," Walter said.

The ranger nodded. "You get any good hiking in?"

"Yeah, we went up the High Peaks Trail yesterday."

"See any condors up there?"

I shook my head. "No, sir. No condors this trip. Just turkey vultures and a couple of falcons."

"And some Germans," Walter added.

The ranger didn't seem surprised. "Yeah, they're up there, but they can be pretty tough to spot." He wasn't talking about the Germans. "Tell you what, if you boys really want to see condors, you might try the Grand Canyon next time."

"To see the California condor?" I said.

"They've got a lot of them out there."

He nodded goodbye and whistled as he lumbered over to the ranger station.

We got back in the car and drove out of the park. The road back to LA was rural at first—and at times there was only one lane going in each direction. We'd been on the road for about fifteen minutes when I saw a flash of feathers dart across the highway and perch on a tree in front of us.

It was a black bird with white on its wings.

I slammed on the brakes. The car came to a screeching halt in the middle of the highway.

"Ian, what the hell are you doing?" Walter yelled. "That's not a condor!"

"I know it isn't," I said, taking off my seatbelt. "It's a yellow-billed magpie. I've never seen one before."

We pulled over to the side of the road and got out. Sure enough, there it was, perched high in the branches of a tree just off the road: a yellow-billed magpie. A gorgeous blue stripe circled its belly like an inner tube. After a few moments, the magpie flew off to continue with its day, and Walter and I got back in the car to continue with ours.

I turned to Walter: "Want to go to the Grand Canyon next week? See if we can spot any California condors in Arizona?"

He smiled. "John'll be better by then so we can drag him along, too."

# NOT THAT

# KIND OF BIRD

Sometimes it's hard to trust your own eyes. When what you see doesn't match your expectations, your brain can play tricks on you. It's hard to know if you're ever actually seeing what you think you are.

I moved to Laurel Canyon after the third season of the show. I'd spend most Sunday mornings playing with my dogs in the yard. The house I lived in backed up to a hill, which Mochi and Bailey would run all over.

Sometimes we'd play fetch, and I'd throw a ball up the slope. They'd tear after it, then trip over their legs as they raced back to me.

Mochi wouldn't always bring back the ball. Sometimes she'd bring a stick instead—and once she brought me a freshly uprooted rosebush.

One such Sunday morning, I let the dogs out and went back inside to get some coffee. The kitchen looked out onto the yard, and I glanced out to see Mochi and Bailey hightailing it after a squirrel.

I grabbed some half-and-half out of the fridge, then looked back out the window again to make sure the dogs weren't getting into trouble. All three of them were romping around, tails wagging.

Wait—what the hell? I only have two dogs.

I leaned over the sink to get a better look outside. There weren't three dogs in the yard. There was Mochi. There was Bailey. And there was a coyote chasing them.

I bolted out the door, waving my arms and shouting. I grabbed a shovel on the ground next to a recently replanted rosebush and ran to save my two helpless dogs from this vicious apex predator.

As I crossed the yard, all three of them—Mochi, Bailey, and the coyote—stopped what they were doing and stared at me. The coyote sniffed the air, then ran off into the bushes. Bailey looked at me and whined.

The coyote hadn't been trying to eat them. He had been playing with them!

The dogs had made a new friend, and I had chased him off with a shovel.

I set the shovel down and called the dogs over. I had been right to scare the coyote off. Coyotes are dangerous. They eat cats and maim dogs . . . and they had looked so happy playing together in the yard.

"Come on, guys. Let's go inside." I ushered the dogs into the house, stopping at the door to take one last look around in case their coyote friend had come back. He had totally vanished.

A few Sundays later, I was again out in the backyard with the dogs. The coyote hadn't come back to visit yet, but I'd been keeping an eye out for him.

As I stood there, waiting for Mochi and Bailey to quit wrestling over a ball and bring it back to me, I spotted a small bird perched out on a dead branch of an oak tree. It was mostly black—it looked like a little flycatcher.

Some flycatchers are notoriously difficult to identify. There's a family of about a dozen of them, called the *Empidonax* flycatchers, which are nearly indistinguishable. Early naturalists would kill birds they were studying in order to see them up close, but killing an empid for identification purposes would be nearly pointless—the only way to reliably tell them apart is their song. And, to add to the fun, if *Empidonax* flycatchers aren't at their summer breeding grounds, they don't sing.

Anyway, those flycatchers are mostly gray, and this bird was mostly black, so I didn't need to worry about its song. The bird sallied out from the branch and caught a bug in midair, then returned to its perch.

My first inclination was that it was a black phoebe, a fairly common type of flycatcher that nested in the neighborhood. But the bird wasn't that far away, and with my naked eye I could see it had a crimson breast and patches of white on the wings.

I watched as the bird skated around the trunk of the tree,

flashing white feathers on the sides of its tail. I was looking for field marks—parts of the bird that are characteristic markers to help distinguish it from other species. The bird I was looking at now had what looked like little white bags under its eyes—giving it an oddly sleep-deprived appearance.

Black phoebes don't have any of these features. They're all black with a white breast.

It suddenly dawned on me that I was looking at an extremely rare bird for Los Angeles: a painted redstart.

Mochi dropped a broom at my feet and began whining. Not wanting to take my eyes off the redstart, I tried to shush her as I backpedaled toward the house to grab a pair of binoculars, maybe even a camera. The bird was spiraling up through the branches of the tree.

I got to the door and dashed inside—but in that short interval, the bird disappeared. By the time I got back outside, I couldn't find it again. I'd seen it for just the briefest of moments—so short that I could barely believe my own eyes.

After searching the trees in my yard for a good half an hour, and then walking up and down the street, I gave up and went back inside. I knew what I'd seen, but I pulled out a bird book to confirm it anyway. I found the right page in the book and checked all the field marks. It was definitely a painted redstart. I was sure of it.

Where was Sophia? Out working?! Damnit. I needed to high-five someone.

That night, I met up with my buddy Walter at a bar in Highland Park. I'd told him I had some really exciting news to share, and he was just about the only person I knew who'd understand how excited I was to have seen a painted redstart in my yard.

"Bullshit," he said, putting down his beer.

"I swear to God," I told him.

"I thought exciting news meant you'd won the lottery, or booked a film, or . . . something that was actually true."

"I'm not making this up! Why would I make this up?"

Walter shook his head. "Did you take a picture?"

"I didn't have time—but it had the red belly, the white patches on the wings . . ."

"Maybe you saw a black phoebe and it caught the light in a weird way."

I'd expected Walter to be just as excited as I was, but now he was trashing my birding abilities.

"You're just jealous," I said, exasperated.

"I'm not jealous, I swear. I think you're just a little overenthusiastic about birds—and you thought you saw something that wasn't actually what you were seeing. Painted redstarts only pop up around here once every few years."

"But they do pop up!"

Walter finished off his beer with a big gulp. "When you were a kid, did you tell everyone you'd seen Santa Claus at your house? Did you lie about that, too?" he asked.

We agreed to talk about something else.


Walter and I had that conversation about two years ago, and to this day, whenever he doesn't believe something I'm saying, he'll ask, "Is this another one of your redstart stories?"

It's easy to misidentify birds when they zip by in the woods and you only glimpse them for a few seconds. But it isn't just birds—or coyotes. We do the same thing with people.

Ever since *Pretty Little Liars* started airing, people have come up to me in restaurants and bars to tell me they recognize me from somewhere. They know they've seen my face, but they can't place it. They'll ask if I went to their church, or if we went to high school together back in Minnesota.

One time I was at a restaurant in Los Feliz called the Alcove. It's got a big outdoor patio area under a few giant oak trees. As I was finishing up my lunch, I heard a muffled gasp from the table behind me. I looked around, and out of the corner of my eye I saw two teenage girls staring at me. One of them had her hand over her mouth. The girls were clearly fans of the show, and I heard them start to argue.

"It's him!" one of them whispered, under her breath.

"There's no way."

"It is! It's definitely him."

I turned back to my food and tried to stop eavesdropping, but I could hear the girls continuing their debate over whether I was actually me. Finally, the one who insisted that I was "him" whispered, "Look at his hair. It *is* him."

"Actually," the friend said. "I think you might be right."

"Told you so."

"Oh my God. What do we do? Do we say something? Should we say hi?"

"No! Don't be an idiot. Leave him alone."

The friend, now fully convinced, wasn't backing down. "I'm going to go over and talk to him," she said.

"Don't!" the first girl hissed.

At this point, I was beginning to feel bad. I felt like my presence in this café was becoming an issue. I quickly paid my bill and stood up to go.

As I did, both girls fell silent and pretended to look the other way. They were smiling.

I couldn't resist. As I passed by them, I leaned in and whispered, "It *is* me."

The girls flipped out.

"Oh my God!" the first one cried, shaking her hands by the side of her face.

"Holy shit!" the friend squealed. "You have no idea how much this means to us. I'm like—I'm your biggest fan, Mr. Marsden."

Oh no. Oh shit.

I'm not James Marsden.

I tried to set the record straight as smoothly as possible.

"I'm so sorry," I said. "I'm—my name's Ian. Ian Harding. I am an actor, but I'm not . . . I'm not who you think I am."

The girls' faces immediately fell. Their smiles vanished.

"I'm on a TV show. It's called—you know what, never mind, doesn't matter."

This was not going well.

"Look, I'm sorry for the confusion. I didn't mean to lead you on."

A voice in my head whispered: *Your name is Ian Harding. You are thirty years old. And right now you are apologizing for not being James Marsden.*

I couldn't think of anything else to say, so I excused myself and left the two crestfallen teenagers to finish their meal in peace.

Nowadays, when people come up to me and say they know me from somewhere but they can't quite place it, I tell them I just have one of those faces.

One of those James Marsden-y faces.

# 'SPLORES

## WITH KEEGAN

Keegan Allen, dear friend, costar, and photographer extraordinaire, sat across from me at Dialog Cafe, a small family-run spot in West Hollywood, just down the street from the more intimidatingly named Viper Room and Rockhard Films.

"So how long's this video need to be?" he asked.

"Only like six seconds. You can shoot it on your phone."

"So I don't need any of these today?" He pointed to three cameras hanging around his neck.

I had told him we were going hiking, and that on the hike we would have to take photos that I had to post on Instagram. Keegan dressed appropriately, while I, on the other hand, had opted not to shave or sleep the night before.

We polished off our now watery iced coffees. Looking out the window, I took in the traffic on Sunset Boulevard. Houses dotted the hills above us, and the sunshine was finally cutting through the June Gloom.

In the café, we were surrounded by young parents, all of whom seemed to be shockingly well rested. The shop was crowded with baby strollers, but none of the babies had cried even once. They all just lay there with these eerily serene looks on their calm faces. Can babies get Botox, I wondered? Maybe they couldn't cry.

Several patrons sat with open laptops resting next to half-eaten pastries. Screenwriters most likely. Or accountants. Or anyone really, but I always assume that if you're in a café with a laptop open, you're probably writing the next *Jaws*.

"Thanks again for helping me shoot this," I said.

"Of course, man." Keegan wiped the lens of his Leica. "And don't feel bad about doing this stuff for money. Everyone does it. Besides, you're helping your family, and in a few months no one will remember or care about a little video you shot in the woods."

I'd been having second thoughts about this photo shoot since the moment I signed on. I was beginning to worry that my social media page might someday look like the side of a race car—plastered with ads and logos, having little if anything to do with the personality of the page's original creator. It was a scary thought.

"How are you getting the photos to the company that hired you?" Keegan asked.

"I think I'll probably just email them over. I can do that right?"

Keegan sighed dramatically. "Oh thank God, Ian. I thought you were about to say passenger pigeon."

"Hilarious. First off, those are extinct. Second, you're thinking of a homing pigeon, which are actually still used—"

"Did people ever actually ride those?"

"..."

"Like, passenger pigeons. Back in the day. Could they ever actually ride them? Like how big were they? Were they—" He spread his arms out wide. "Were they bus-sized?"

"Are you asking me if *The Flintstones* happened in real life?"

Keegan stared at me in silence for a moment then downed the remainder of his iced coffee.

Here's a sentence I don't always like to say out loud: I have a branding agent. Her name is Jean Kwolek, and she's lovely.

Jean attaches her clients—mostly actors—to various commercial campaigns, which supplement their income between acting gigs. Look really good with three-day stubble? She can help you sell whiskey. Never had dandruff? Easy: hair commercials. It isn't always that blatant, either. There are increasingly lucrative ways for people in the public eye to make a little dough on the side without looking like total sellouts.

That's an interesting word, by the way. I struggle with it constantly: sellout. The term has always carried a strange gravity in my mind, and it was echoing back and forth in my head that day. I felt a bit off using my acting for purely financial gain.

But, two months earlier, my sister Sarah had been granted a slot in a highly selective Directors Guild training program in

New York. Both she and I had rejoiced at the news of this opportunity, but our rejoicing quickly came to an end when we began to consider how she would pay for it. Sarah would be working as a PA in New York, and would have a couple of hours here and there to Uber or walk dogs on the side, but she wouldn't be making nearly enough money to support herself in New York City.

For Sarah, this opportunity was a dream come true. I gave it some thought, and I decided to play fairy god-brother. I called my sister and told her I wanted to cover her rent for the two years she would be living in the Big Apple. That way she could focus entirely on learning and working in the field she's always loved. The news brought tears to her eyes, and when I told my accountant about it, she nearly cried as well.

After I told Sarah that I intended to cover her rent, I immediately emailed Jean and my manager, Vikram. I asked them to find me campaign work—anything they could find that didn't involve an actual deal with the devil.

"So how far away is this waterfall?" Keegan asked, holding one of his cameras up to the window and snapping away at the passing scenery.

We were driving along the Angeles Crest Highway as it wound its way up from La Cañada Flintridge through the Angeles National Forest. We were headed to Switzer Falls.

"Can't be more than another twenty minutes or so."

"Did they say why they wanted this waterfall in particular?"

"No, it was my idea. The company just needs me to tape myself having fun. I told them I wanted to do a hike because it's something I actually do."

A short while later, I spotted our turn and hung a sharp right. We passed some serious-looking road spikes and proceeded down a winding hill toward Switzer Falls.

The last time I went on this hike was in 2014. It had been a wettish winter—not wet enough to break the drought, but it was a welcome change for us—and the falls had taken on the appearance of, well, actual waterfalls. I had hiked out early one morning after a late winter rain with a few friends from college. The falls had bellowed loudly as we approached them at the end of the trail. I had put my head under, and the force of the water blew off my hat.

That was then. This was now. And by "now" I mean it was a Tuesday in July, and the weather service was predicting another day of record-breaking heat.

We pulled into a parking spot by a picnic table.

"It looks pretty parched out here. Are you sure there's any water going over the falls right now?" Keegan asked.

I wasn't.

"Push comes to shove, I have a gallon of water in the back of my car and maybe you can just pour that over my head? Then like, throw some leaves at me?"

"Sure, man. I could do that."

We walked over to the trailhead. Ten yards from the start of the hike, a man slowly walked by us, carrying a walking stick. His face was stoic, lost deep in thought. I recognized him. I looked to Keegan, who had noticed him as well. We kept walking, paying more attention than necessary to the trees above our heads, overcompensating in our attempt not to disturb the wistful hiker.

A hundred yards down the trail, Keegan and I, now alone, turned to each other and simultaneously said: "Moby."

I was a huge Moby fan in high school. His music got me through puberty. I've even used Moby songs to prepare for auditions.

"Crazy. Of all the places," I said.

"What are you talking about?" Keegan asked. "Moby belongs in the forest. If we'd bumped into him at, like, Bed Bath & Beyond, that would have been weird."

I turned and looked back up the trail toward the parking lot.

"I kind of wish we had said something."

Keegan laughed. "Well, we can always creep over and watch him from one of those trees with your binoculars if you want."

I stopped in my tracks. I pictured my binoculars, my little Nikons, sitting on my kitchen counter. I'd forgotten them at home.

"Damnit!" I yelled.

My expletive echoed through the canyon, scaring birds from their nests. Birds that I could have seen, if I'd remembered my binoculars.

"Everything okay?" Keegan asked.

"I forgot my binoculars."

"I'm not sure forgetting your binoculars warrants that kind of response." His voice sounded like a high school guidance counselor's.

He was right. I had promised him a short jaunt in the woods.

I hadn't said anything about birding. Still, the anxious bird-nerd in me worried that I might spot something and not be able to get a good look at it.

We continued onward, sans specs.

The trail to Switzer Falls is a four-and-half-mile trek—out and back—with several other paths forking out from it along the way. It starts pleasantly enough: there's a small paved section of the path for the first third of a mile. Eventually the road tapers off into a dirt-and-rock-strewn trail. Several streams intersect the path until roughly the mile-and-a-half marker. Then the trail snakes upward, away from the water. This section continues for some time, rising slowly, before the trail turns back down, leading to a forested canyon.

In the middle of the canyon, there's a sign that states—dauntingly—TRAIL NOT MAINTAINED.

It's not actually that rough. What the sign should say is, THERE'S STILL A TRAIL. DON'T WORRY. JUST FOLLOW THE FOOTPRINTS ON THE GROUND AND THE SOUND OF THE FALLING WATER AND YOU SHOULD BE ALL GOOD. HEADS UP, THOUGH: THERE ARE A COUPLE OF FALLEN LOGS NEAR THE END SO LOOK OUT FOR THOSE.

A lot of people turn around at the TRAIL NOT MAINTAINED sign. But if you keep going, you get to see Switzer Falls in all their glory. And they are worth it. The falls themselves are about fifty feet high. The water shoots out from the top, hitting a landing about halfway down and splashing out in all directions. At the base of the falls is a swimming hole when there's enough water.

Because not everyone makes it past the TRAIL NOT MAIN-
TAINED sign, the falls are usually deserted, especially on week-
days. It's a wonderful place to get away and clear your mind, as
Moby apparently knows as well.

There was a thwack thwack thwack above our heads. Something was making a racket.

Keegan looked to the canopy, scanning bare limbs and
dead branches. "That's a woodpecker I'm guessing?" he asked.

"You're right, though it's a little too high up to see what kind."

"What kinds live around here?"

I couldn't tell if Keegan truly cared or was simply asking
out of politeness.

"There are a few different species. Maybe three or four."

"What are their names? How do you tell them apart—by
the noise they make?"

"Yeah, sometimes."

I don't know why I felt shy. I knew the answers to his questions. I turned and looked at Keegan. He seemed genuinely
curious.

"You're really not supposed to do this, because it messes
with the wildlife, but check this out."

I pulled out my phone and opened the Sibley bird app. I
typed "woodpecker" into the search bar. Twelve options came
up. Judging by our altitude and the type of forest we were in—
and the fact that a few of the dead trees around us had an unmistakable honeycomb pattern running up their sides—I had
an idea of what the racket above might be. I opened the page
titled "Acorn Woodpecker."

"Watch this," I said.

I hit play. My phone emitted a series of shrieks and cackles high into the forest canopy. It sounded like a gaggle of angry clowns at a young child's last birthday party before he embarked on a lifetime of therapy.

The recording came to an end and a few seconds passed. We stood around, waiting for something to happen.

A few feet away, there was an oak tree with a dead branch protruding from its side. Though the sun illuminated the length of it, neither of us had noticed the branch until now. A sudden flicker of shadow fell across the top of it. I blinked, and suddenly there they were: three acorn woodpeckers, perched not twenty feet away from us, their beady yellow eyes fixed on my phone.

I held the phone over my head, then pressed play again on the same recording.

The three birds shot toward us, missing our heads by inches. Keegan's hair was blown to the side by the wake of their flight. They cackled as they disappeared into the woods.

"That was amazing!" Keegan said, slapping me on the back. He was clearly impressed by my cellphone's godlike ability to call the birds down from the treetops.

I suddenly felt silly for feeling shy earlier. Keegan and I have worked through breakups together, the passing of family members, and—perhaps most memorably—the near death of his beloved cat Minin from ingested hair ties. Birds shouldn't have been a big deal.

"Can we do it again?" he asked. "That was sick. Do you have any other animals on there? Like, could we call some deer or something?"

"Yeah, let's get some bears over here while we're at it. Maybe even call in a few rattlesnakes. We'll have a party!"

Keegan's smile evaporated. "Wait, but, not really though, right?"

"No, not really. It's a bird app. It's only birds. And we probably shouldn't do that again, anyway."

We stood there for a moment. Keegan seemed a little disappointed.

I took a few steps down the trail, then turned around. "I didn't know you were afraid of snakes," I said.

"Hate 'em."

"When did that start?"

"When I was a kid. I had few encounters with them, and they were never good. One time, I was driving in the car with my mom, and a snake came up to the passenger side and tried to eat our tire. That was it for me, man. I was done. I know everyone always says, 'They're more afraid of you than you are of them,' but that's bullshit, man. If that thing wasn't afraid of a Chevy, why the hell would it be scared of me?"

We continued to talk as we made our way up the shaded canyon to the falls. As we walked, Keegan snapped a few shots of me. I couldn't remember if the company wanted me to do any other media—all I remembered was they wanted a video— so a few extra pictures of me out in nature looking sexy and mildly confused couldn't hurt.

We heard the falls before we saw them. Magically, there was still some water spilling down to a small pond at the base.

Keegan pulled out his phone. "Get over there, man. Time to sell your soul."

I scrambled around the rocks to the base of the falls, and called back to Keegan:

"You ready?"

"Do it!" he yelled.

I dunked my head underwater and then whipped it back, sending a rainbow of glistening droplets into the air.

Willow Smith has a song about whipping her hair back and forth—it should come with a disclaimer. Whipping your hair back and forth is painful: the result is less fun and fancy-free and more dizzy and neck pain-y.

Keegan, standing about thirty feet away, called out, "Do it again, man. I didn't catch that one."

Time for take two. I doused my head in the pond and let it soak for a moment. Then, really selling it this time, I whipped my hair back up and out of the water. I felt something pop—in my shoulder, of all places—and I rolled sideways into a pile of rotting wood.

Keegan remained where he was, squinting at the screen of his iPhone.

"Did you get it?" I asked, still lying on the ground.

He shook his head. "Let's try it again."

I resumed my position on all fours above the puddle at the foot of the falls, and whipped back once more. And then again. After a few more takes, Keegan stopped me.

"Can I ask you something?" he said.

"Shoot."

"Why are you so set on this? They said you can do anything, right? Why not do something that doesn't involve soaking your head in giardia?"

He had a good point. I stood and brushed off my knees. "I

don't know. It's like a ritual, I guess. I have this thing that I do whenever I go on a hike—I've done it since I was a kid. If I see a body of water at the end of the hike, I just have to dunk my head into it."

"Like a baptism?" Keegan's face looked a bit incredulous.

"I guess. Like a cleansing thing."

Keegan squinted at the phone again then looked back at me. "Dude haven't you already been baptized enough?"

"I don't know. I want to make it at least seem authentic. I don't want it to look like I'm not trying. If I have to sell something, I at least want to make it matter. So I want to do my little ritual, and I know it's stupid, but I want to pay homage, I guess, to the woods. Or something. But looking at it now, I realize we're in a drought, and bathing in a waterfall when there's a drought doesn't really seem right."

Keegan looked serious.

"I hear you, man. But honestly this is as authentic as you're going to get. You freaking hiked here. You made me hike here. For a four-second video for—what does the company do again?"

"Online music sharing."

"Yeah, for online music sharing. That's not half-assing it. That's full-assing it. I mean that's a whole lot of ass, Ian. You've got more ass than I'll ever have."

"Because I'm fat?"

"Yeah. Because you're fat," he said, smiling. "Now get your fat, horrible face back into that waterfall and let's send your sister to band camp."

"It's not band camp, Keegan—"

"Back in the waterfall!"

I dunked my head back into the pond, and Keegan circled around, trying to find the best angle for the shot. After a few more takes, I started hopping around the rocks, striking superhero poses for the camera and trying my best to balance on one leg.

"Try to look thoughtful. Like high school yearbook-y," Keegan hollered over the sound of the falls.

I raised one leg and put it on a rock in front of me. I tilted my head a little and tried to look pensive. My back leg started to slip, and I looked down to catch myself. As I looked down, I noticed that I was not the only thing basking on the rocks that afternoon. I jumped backward and jogged over to Keegan.

"What's up?" he said, putting down the phone.

"Want to see something cool?"

His face fell, and his voice grew small. "There's a snake in those rocks, isn't there?"

"Yes. Yes there is."

He closed his eyes and took a deep breath. His fists were clenched, knuckles white. We stood in silence for a moment, listening to the soft patter of the falls behind us. The birds in the trees around us were quiet, seemingly awaiting our next move.

I looked back at the rocks to see if there was any movement. The snake seemed to be lying low.

"It's not in the path," I said. "We can easily go around—"

"Nah, let's do this."

Keegan swung a camera from around his back into his right hand. He looked like a gunslinger from the Old West. He approached the rocks with a steady pace, showing neither apprehension nor glee.

I tried to stop him. "Hey Keegan, I'm pretty sure this was like day one of Boy Scouts. You know, 'Hi Ian, nice to meet you. You'll be in Rabbit Troop. Don't touch snakes!'"

He kept walking, completely resolved to the task. He placed his foot on top of the small boulder where mine had been moments before, and peered over, raising his camera to his eyes as though the lens were a shield.

He looked over the top of the stone and saw the snake.

At this point, several things might have happened. One option—a very viable one—was for Keegan to see the snake, let out a bloodcurdling scream, and run for the hills. Another option was for the snake to bite Keegan. Or perhaps he could have stomped on the snake in a fit of fear-fueled rage.

What I absolutely did not expect, though, was to see Keegan's face go from slight fear to unguarded sadness. His brow furrowed, and he lowered his camera as he stepped over the rocks.

I walked up and looked over his shoulder as he knelt before the motionless reptile.

The snake was dead. When it was alive, it had been a California kingsnake, a beautifully patterned nonvenomous snake native to this part of the world. People keep them as pets, and they're supposed to be quite affectionate.

There were several wounds around the kingsnake's head and neck. It had been in a fight with something, maybe a rock squirrel, and it had lost.

Keegan couldn't take his eyes off it. "Maybe it's a good sign that this actually makes me really sad," he said. "You know what I mean?"

I nodded. We stood there for a few moments, arrested by

the sight of the gentle-looking snake. Keegan slowly rose and turned back to the falls, leaving the snake where it lay.

After a moment, he regained his composure. "How about you jump over the pond like you did when you saw that snake and I'll try and take a video of it," he said, smiling again.

I walked back to the tiny pool, rubbing my neck at the thought of my previous video attempts.

"Do you think I could look sexy jumping?"

Keegan put the camera down. "Ian, no one looks sexy jumping. Just do it."

The route back to the parking lot was the same as the one we had taken to get to the falls. It took longer getting back, though. I stopped to examine every chirp and drum in the trees above—despite having forgot my binoculars. Keegan scaled the hillsides, cameras swinging from the straps across his shoulders, in search of the perfect nature shot. I felt like I was back in the woods behind my house in Virginia, playing with my friends and making up stories about the world around us.

Our conversation, like our journey back, wandered to and fro. We talked about relationships, about altruism, about what it really means to love somebody more than you loved yourself. We talked about butts, too. And how they're awesome.

As my car came into view, Keegan turned to me.

"So we're going to be done in October," he said. "No more *Pretty Little Liars*."

"Yup," I said. "It's almost over."

I opened the back of my station wagon—a car Keegan at first ridiculed but now adores—and sat under the lift gate. I took off my damp boots, allowing my feet to dry in the mountain breeze. Keegan sat next to me.

"You know what I'm looking forward to?" he said.

"What?"

"Having someone come up to me and say, 'Hey, weren't you that guy from *Pretty Little Liars*?'"

"Why are you excited about that?" I asked.

"Because that will mean the show is done. I like the show, don't get me wrong. I don't want it to end, but it will be nice to finally get to look at it in hindsight, you know? Try and wrap my mind around the whole thing. You can't do that when you're in it."

I hadn't thought about it like that. Saying goodbye to *PLL* had never felt like an opportunity to me. For me, it had always felt like an ending—and as I often do with endings, I tried not to think about it too much.

But now, in a parking lot in the middle of the mountains, in wet socks and sweaty clothes, I actually began to think about this chapter of my life coming to an end.

It's difficult to describe. It's similar to the pain you experience when reading a book that has really moved you. You feel the pages thinning as you near the back cover. You love the book, so you want to keep reading, but you know that the more you read the closer you are to being finished, to not getting to read that book for the first time again. I began to choke up.

We sat there for a moment. Sweating. Thinking.

Keegan turned to me. "We should do stuff like this more often. Especially when we're unemployed in a few months."

I closed the trunk and got into the car. Keegan climbed into the passenger seat.

"Yeah," I said. "I'd like to hike a whole lot more. It's like meditating, but, you know, with more birds."

"No. I mean we should do more social media posts for money. I want to stave off having to do porn for as long as possible."

# AND ALL
# THE BIRDS AT SEA

Late last June, I had the morning off from shooting, and I wanted to get out of the house.

I called up John and Walter the night before, hoping they were both free. Walter was wrapping up a writing project but said he could take the morning off. John huffed at me over the phone—he said he'd been planning to color-coordinate his massive book collection the following day.

"What did you want to do?" he hollered over the Chopin that was booming in the background.

"Let's go down to the beach in San Pedro, find a local brewery . . ."

"I'm listening," he said.

"Maybe we could even peruse a bookshop or two," I said, trying to rouse the bibliophile in him.

"Fine," he said. "I'll make an exception this time, as long as we stop at a bookstore."

Before I got off the phone with him, he had one last question. I couldn't hear him over the music he had playing, so he had to repeat it a few times.

"There aren't going to be any birds on this trip, right?" he finally shouted into the phone.

"Nope, not at all. It's a beach day," I hollered back.

It wasn't a beach day. There'd been reports of a brown booby down in San Pedro—I'd never seen one before, and I thought it would make a good half-day trip to try and find it.

Yes, that's right, I was hoping to get a good look at a brown booby.

Despite what you might be thinking, boobies aren't named for their pendulous breasts. The word "booby" comes from the Spanish *bobo*, meaning clown or idiot.

Most birds, when humans get too close, fly away. Boobies are different. They're curious, and they're clumsy. Boobies will land on sailing ships and toddle around the decks like buffoons—they'll even wander up to people to see what *Homo sapiens* are all about.

Because they land on ships, they're particularly easy to catch and eat—so humans took the birds' innate curiosity as an opportunity to brand them as stupid. It's a little bit like what happened to the dodo: when animals aren't overtly aggressive or fearful, humans assume they're slow in the head.

I had to keep the purpose of the trip to myself when I picked up John. I swung by his house a little before six the next morning, and he came outside in a bathrobe. I thought he'd just woken up, but he tried to get into the car and insisted he was ready to go—I refused to unlock the car doors until he changed into regular clothes.

After he did so, we grabbed Walter, who was waiting outside his apartment with a thermos of coffee and extra paper cups for the road.

As we coasted down the highway to San Pedro, the three of us still slowly waking up, Walter piped up from the backseat:

"I wonder what our chances are of seeing the booby first thing in the morning."

John's whole body swiveled to face me.

"The booby?" he asked. "Like the blue-footed booby?"

"Oh, so you know what we're talking about then," I said.

"Yeah, I know. The last time I saw one was in the Galápagos."

"Well, that's pretty cool," I said.

"A sea lion tried to mate with me."

Hesitantly, I offered, "Well, technically, we're trying to find the brown booby today—they're closely related."

John was not pleased.

"I thought you said there wouldn't be any birds—"

"We'll be on the beach, it'll be beautiful and sunny, and we can jump in the water. After that we'll go find a bookstore," I said, not sure if any of the things I had just promised were true.

San Pedro is technically a part of the City of Los Angeles, but driving in, it felt like a different world—it was originally a small fishing village but is now a part of the Port of Los Angeles, the largest port in the United States. Massive cranes line the channel that juts inland just east of the city, and cargo ships stream in and out, loaded to the brim with shipping containers.

As we got closer to the coast, it began to get cloudy, then very cloudy, then completely overcast. It didn't look like weather for sun-tanning, or even beach-going. That morning it'd been sunny back home in East LA, but now it was clouds as far as the eye could see. It was at least ten degrees cooler outside, too.

John told us he had spent some time in the town before when he was auditioning for the role of Creon in an immersive production of *Oedipus Rex* put on by a band of local fishermen. He said he knew a good spot for breakfast.

As we sat around eating bagels and sipping our second cups of coffee for the day, Walter pulled out his phone to see if there were any new rare bird alerts about the booby that morning. It was still early, and there weren't any.

After breakfast, we headed to the coast—to an overlook people had seen the booby from before. Watching the frothing waves of the Pacific wash up against the rocky shore reminded me of New England.

The sky was the same distinctive gray you get on the East Coast. Like dull smoke, it blended seamlessly with the waves on the horizon—a wash of ashy steel as far as the eye could see.

The three of us walked along the overlook, gazing out at the water. There wasn't much going on bird-wise. The only thing of interest was a group of sad-faced fishermen bobbing up and down on a ship called the *Monte Carlo*. Way off to our left was the port, where cranes were speedily transferring shipping containers off vessels.

There were a few seagulls. Terns. Pelicans flying low over the water. The usual.

"There's a Jesus egret out there," Walter said. He'd been scanning the water with his binoculars.

"What? Where?" I asked. "What's a Jesus egret?"

Walter pointed out toward what may have been the horizon—I couldn't quite tell where the water ended and the sky began.

"That speck of white out there, way in the distance—check it out," he said.

Sure enough, way, way out I could see an egret standing on a raft of kelp and seaweed. The bird took a cautious step forward—it was hunting for small fish or crustaceans.

"See, it's walking on water," Walter said.

Behind us, John groaned loudly.

I looked at the egret for another second or two, then turned back to the guys.

"What do you think?" I asked. "Seems pretty slow out there—definitely no boobies."

John pointed a little up the coast at some spray-painted structures on the side of a cliff.

"Want to check over there?" he asked.

As we walked toward the spray-painted buildings, we passed an old woman on a park bench who was feeding stray cats like they were pigeons. Five cats gathered around her, meowing and vibrating with feral purrs.

As we passed her, I wondered, would that be me someday? Would I end up an old cat lady, too? It was a definite possibility. But she seemed happy enough—and so did the cats. Maybe being a cat lady would be fun.

We walked through the neighborhood and wandered behind the houses to see if there was an open gate somewhere. Nothing.

About a hundred yards away, a man was walking around inside the fenced-off enclosure. He climbed up onto what appeared to be a partially collapsed roof. I took out my binoculars to get a closer look.

The man bent down and adjusted the cuffs of his pants. Then, slowly, the man sat down to face the ocean and began to meditate. I could see his back rising and falling with deep, mindful breaths.

I felt a tap on my shoulder. It was John.

"Check it out," he said, and he carefully pushed my binoculars down and to the right so that I was suddenly making eye contact with a mostly bald, mostly angry Chihuahua seated just next to the man on the roof—keeping guard while his master meditated. The Chihuahua glared unblinkingly at me from across the fence, daring me to even consider interrupting his master's solo time.

We kept walking for a few minutes and eventually found a gap in the fence. Someone had pried off one of the iron bars and replaced it with a bit of iron-colored wood. We squeezed through the fence and stepped into what I would later learn was San Pedro's Sunken City.

The Sunken City was a real estate development that started with a visionary's dream in the early 1920s but ended with a landslide less than a decade later. The landslide was gradual, but devastating. In January of 1929, the pace picked up considerably. The ground underneath the entire development started shifting down toward the water at a rate of roughly eleven inches per day. Residents paid to have their houses moved farther inland, but a few of them weren't moved in time. The houses began to slide off the muddy cliff and into the waves below.

Nine months later, the stock market crashed, plunging the country into the worst depression its ever faced. Any plans of salvaging the quickly vanishing development were abandoned, and the remaining structures were left to slide into the sea at their own pace.

Nowadays, high school kids and local gangs take over the Sunken City at night. But during the day it's just a sad collection of collapsed rooftops and empty concrete structures with dirt paths winding between them.

We shuffled down a steep incline and into the center of the Sunken City. Walter and I headed to the cliff overlooking the ocean while John hung back to look at graffiti. We didn't see many shorebirds, and definitely no boobies, but we did pass a group of seven or eight teenagers who looked like they were straight out of the movie *Warriors*. I don't know if they were actually a gang, but if they were, I have to say that they were remarkably cordial, and I'm impressed that they hold their gang meetings at 8:30 on Wednesday mornings. It's not every gang you see that can really master the breakfast meeting.

We walked past the roof where the man had been meditating a few minutes before. He was gone, along with his guard Chihuahua.

Walter was scanning the horizon for shorebirds. John was trying to read a graffiti-ed love note on the underside of an old roof. I decided to go off on my own for a moment.

The man I'd seen meditating on the rooftop had looked so peaceful, so serene, that I wanted to take a crack at it myself. I climbed up on the same concrete rooftop he'd been on, crossed my legs and closed my eyes. I started to take slow deep breaths.

I listened to the waves, to the sound of John's voice as he tried to decipher the spray paint on the walls, to the sounds of a well-organized gang meeting in the distance. I heard footsteps nearby, and I opened my eyes.

Walter stood below me on a precarious-looking slab that angled downward toward the sea. His binoculars hung from his shoulder, a sign that there was little to see.

We began to wonder if it was legal for us to be wandering around the Sunken City. Squeezing between the bars of a fence tends to fall under the header of "trespassing," so we started walking back to where we'd snuck in. On our way, we found a different break in the fence that spit us out into a park. We walked along the perimeter, which had views to the ocean, and observed a couple of bored-looking seagulls and two more feral cats. A group of old people threw some bread their way as we walked by.

San Pedro needs to stop treating its cats like pigeons.

Finding nothing but cats and seagulls, we headed to the car.

"Sorry about the waste of a morning, guys," I said, as I turned the key in the ignition.

"We could still go somewhere else," Walter said. He didn't seem ready to give up quite yet on the booby.

"What about the shipwreck?" John said from the backseat. He was looking at his phone.

"What shipwreck?" I asked.

"Apparently there's a shipwreck thirty minutes from here. It could be cool."

Walter looked at me and shrugged. "Let's check it out."

When we got to Palos Verdes, the closest town to the wreck, the first thing we noticed was the view. The sky had parted, and the sun illuminated the beach.

We got lost in a neighborhood trying to find the path down to the shipwreck, finally parking along the ocean across from a few palatial estates. On the other side of the road, the ocean sparkled in the light. We had arrived on the edge of a cliff, and a picturesque beach lay a hundred feet below. Wave-smoothed rocks lined the shore—and there didn't seem to be an easy way to get down to them.

We agreed to split up and try to find a trail down. Walter went to the left and peered over a ledge. Then without much fanfare, he jumped.

John and I, wondering if our friend had just casually killed himself, sprinted over to see what had become of him. Walter had landed roughly ten feet below, on a rocky outcrop on the cliff face. He waved to us, then skidded down on his heels to about the halfway point of the wall. He motioned for us to slide down and join him, but neither John nor I liked our odds of survival on the near-vertical cliff face, so we kept walking to see if there was a slightly more gradual trail available.

As we walked along, John started humming a tune that I quickly recognized as "One Headlight" by the Wallflowers.

"Please stop that," I said. I tried to walk faster so I could get away from him.

It was too late. Certain songs are earworms. They enter your ear, innocently at first, then get stuck in the core of your brain, and nothing can shake them out.

By the time we found a trail down the cliff, John and I were both several verses in, belting out Jakob Dylan like our lives depended on it.

John started laughing. "He really was the better of the two Dylans," he said.

"Whatever happened to him?"

John shrugged. "I don't know, man. Whatever happened to any of the nineties pop stars? He probably settled down and opened a bike shop somewhere in the Pacific Northwest."

The path we were going down was treacherous, and rocks crumbled beneath our feet as we scrambled our way down to the beach below, where we found Walter patiently waiting.

Sailors can be superstitious folk. To this day, many of them still refuse to set sail on Fridays. They avoid bananas and redheads. They don't like whistling—and not because it's annoying, but because they say it causes storms.

For all of the superstition of sailors, the people who actually name the ships clearly don't buy into the idea of bad luck. I don't know who it was who first spread the rumor that the *Titanic* was unsinkable, but trust me, it wasn't a sailor. Openly advertising that level of hubris is flirting with disaster.

Similarly, naming a ship the SS *Dominator* begs for the

ocean to destroy it. And that is exactly what happened to the SS *Dominator*, a freighter bound for Los Angeles in the spring of 1961—it got dominated.

Nobody died in the wreck. Bad weather drove the ship aground, battering it into the rocks, where it remained. Attempts to pull the boat back out to sea were fruitless. The *Dominator* was then auctioned off, but the new owners weren't able to salvage much.

The coastline is now littered with bits and pieces of rusted freight ship. The larger pieces are bright orange with rust or covered with multiple generations of graffiti. Here and there around the wreckage you can see spiny lobster traps, dented by sea lions that have tried to break through the metal grates in hopes of a free meal.

We stayed down by the shipwreck for a little under an hour. We watched some crabs fight, cast bets on our favorites, hung our heads in disappointment when they reached a truce, and decided to hike back up to the car.

As we walked back up the cliff to the car, I started thinking about the SS *Dominator* and its terribly ironic name. Once a ship runs aground, nobody remembers what it did or what its purpose was; we just remember that it crashed. All we think about is how it ended.

This got me thinking about endings. I was a few months away from ending what, for the past seven years, had been my life. *Pretty Little Liars* would soon be over—I was less than four months away from the end of filming—and I'd been mulling over the coming changes in my life ever since my hike with Keegan.

A few weeks before the trip to San Pedro, my mom had

emailed to ask if I wanted her and Aunt Jules to fly out to LA to celebrate the end of the show—sort of a small family wrap party. She had also asked how I was feeling about the show ending, and I told her I didn't really know yet.

I read somewhere that, when Shakespeare was alive, nobody really liked the plays that we now consider to be his classics. Nowadays, we remember Shakespeare for plays like *Hamlet*, *Macbeth*, and *Othello*. But in his lifetime, those shows weren't the favorites. Everyone kept asking him to write more plays like *Titus Andronicus* and *Pericles*—violent, sex-filled crowd-pleasers.

If someone as gifted and hardworking as Shakespeare didn't get to have any say in the trajectory of his career, what chance do the rest of us have? You could spend thirty years working on Greek tragedies, and all anyone would remember you for was a smoothie commercial.

Thinking all of this, I started to feel guilty. I was lucky to be where I was. It's a rare enough thing to get to make a living as an actor—I knew I needed to stop overthinking it all and just be grateful.

But you can't turn off thoughts like that. They're like Jakob Dylan songs—they just get stuck in your head for hours and hours.

We got back in the car and debated about what to do next.

About a mile down the road, I pulled off at another over-look. Living in LA, I don't get to see the ocean nearly as often as you might expect, and I wanted to get one last look before we headed home.

There was a trail near the turnout, and Walter suggested we go down it a ways to see if there was anything to see.

As we walked, a thought struck me. I turned to Walter. "There are about ten thousand species of birds, right?"

"God, I hope not," John said.

Walter nodded, "Yeah, just about ten thousand."

"Nobody's ever seen them all, have they? Like, that's not possible. Nobody could ever do that."

"You're right," Walter said. "It's probably not possible."

"Because that's not the point of it, right? I mean, even though we try to see as many as we can—and we keep life lists and call each other whenever we see a new bird, it isn't about the numbers. Not seeing every last bird doesn't diminish the joy of birding."

"When you guys *have* seen them all, will you please stop tricking me into going on these birding trips?" John asked. I'd completely forgotten that I'd promised to take him to a bookstore.

We arrived at a bench on the side of the sea, and we sat down. Walter took out his binoculars and scanned the coast. I thought I saw a loon in the distance, but it was too far out to be sure. I thought about my aunt Jules.

A gray blur shot by us. I tracked it with my eyes and turned to follow it but wasn't fast enough. I didn't see where it landed. It had disappeared somewhere in the bushes.

"Did you guys see that?" I asked.

John pointed to some brambles about a hundred feet from us. For someone who claims to hate birds, he's pretty good at spotting them.

Walter perked up. "That's a California gnatcatcher. They're a coastal specialty."

It was the first time I'd ever seen one.

———

We drove back to San Pedro for fish and chips, then headed home.

As we sped along in my station wagon, we talked about taking another trip. John told us he wanted to go to Oregon to do some white-water rafting, and he invited us to join him. I told him it would depend on when I was filming—as the show got closer to ending, my schedule was becoming more erratic.

"Oh yeah," he said. "I forgot about the show ending. How are you feeling about that?"

"You know honestly, I don't know," I said. "Everyone keeps asking me that, and I wish I had a better answer to give. But I'm still in it now. Filming these last couple of episodes hasn't felt any different from filming the rest of the show. I don't feel a loss, or an absence in my life, or anything like that. When I stop filming, then I know I'll start to feel something, but as long as I'm working on it I can't really imagine what it will feel like to say goodbye."

In the backseat, John pulled a pack of Twizzlers out of his backpack and offered them around.

"And I know that once it's done there will be some big changes," I said. "Like my hair. I've been contractually obligated to have the same haircut for the last seven years. Whenever it gets long, I text Kim to see if I can come in during my lunch break to get it trimmed—I'm not supposed to go to anybody else. It will be strange to not have her cut my hair anymore. Or when my chest hair grows back and I don't have to worry about shaving it again for work, then I'll be reminded that the show is really over. That might be when I start to feel nostalgic. Then I'll be sad. But right now, I'm still busy with it. My mind can't be here and four months in the future at the same time, you know?"

Walter nodded. John was quiet for a moment. Then he spoke up.

"When the show's over, can you do me a favor?" he asked.

"Yeah, what's up?"

"Shave your head and grow a mohawk."

When I was a kid, I couldn't count to thirty.

My brain would always skip the number. I'd try really hard to count correctly. I'd start out: "Twenty-eight, twenty-nine . . . forty." Every time. Something about the number eluded me.

When this book is published, I will be halfway through my thirtieth year—a number I could never imagine. It isn't frightening. It isn't thrilling. It doesn't feel that different at all.

The thing about uncharted territory is, once you get there, it just becomes familiar terrain.

I dropped the guys off at their homes in LA. Walter went back to his writing and editing, and John returned to his library and his beloved Chopin records.

As I drove home—my car winding through the hills of East LA—my mind returned to the ocean. We hadn't seen many birds, but I had found myself looking out at the horizon all morning. I was looking for something. I knew, even though I couldn't see them, that there were birds out there.

There's a set of birds called the pelagics. They're the first ones in most birding books: the albatrosses, petrels, shearwaters, and so on. The thing about these birds is most people will never see them. Every bird book starts with pages and pages of pictures of birds that most people will never lay eyes on.

The reason nobody sees these birds is because they never come to us. If you sit in your yard and wait by the feeder your whole life, you'll never spot a pelagic bird. If you want to see one, you'll have to hop in a boat and actually leave the land to meet them on their own turf.

Pelagic birds live at sea, and some species will go five years without ever seeing dry land. Their life is constant movement. They eat while flying. They sleep while flying. When the wind stops, they float in the sea and wait for the next gust, but there's no stopping. They hatch out of their eggs, and once they fledge, they're up in the air for life. An albatross or a shearwater will live for forty years, and every day of that life is spent either floating or flying.

As humans, we tend to crave solid ground. We want stability, comfort. Some of us live our whole lives waiting for that moment when we can say, "Now. Now I'm here. Now I'm where I need to be, and everything's okay."

But not all of us are the same kind of bird.

Some people need to nest. They need to make a place that they can call home, and that's what makes them happy. Others are like falcons: they live for the hunt, for the rush of competition and moments of intense, beautiful conflict.

I think I may be more like one of those pelagics. I can't look forward and say, "There. There is the place where I want to land." My show is ending soon, and with any luck I'll book something new—or I'll just keep flying, waiting for the next gust of wind.

If the goal is to find a comfortable place to perch and watch the world go by, I know that doesn't exist for me. At least not now.

I think the secret to a happy life is to keep moving, to keep trying to do the things you love.

And maybe—just maybe, if you're really lucky—while you're out there flying and flapping for years and years, you'll see some pretty incredible things.

# Acknowledgments

Publishing a book and starring in a television show are shockingly similar; both involve the creation and telling of a story by hundreds of people, for which the lead of that book/show gets all the credit.

Here I wish to thank the many, MANY people without whom this book wouldn't have been possible.

For my ever-loving and ever-supportive family: I owe you all. Thank you for encouraging my imagination over the years, and for showing me that a life on the stage is not only a career, but also a calling.

John McKetta and Walter Heymann, for your support, wisdom, and deep love of all things avian. Especially you, John. . . .

For the Herndon fellows: I miss you all daily. Thank you for the childhood from hell/heaven.

For my *PLL* family: Thank you for an epic seven years. It was an honor to grow with you all.

Scott Mendel, for pushing me to write the book I wanted to write, and for the attentive ear.

Vikram Dhawer, Steve Gersh, Nick Collins, and Kyetay Backner, for your guidance and for giving me the opportunity to chase my dreams.

St. Martin's Press, for taking a chance on an actor with a crazy idea. Most especially thanks to Sara Goodman, for your keen eye and ability to clarify everything I've written. For the rest, Alicia Clancy, Anna Gorovoy, Olga Grlic, Jess Preeg, Laura Clark, Jessalyn Foggy, Meryl Gross, Eva Diaz, and Jim Tierney: thank you for your hard work.

To those of you who have watched *Pretty Little Liars* with the same passion I had in making it: thank you. I would not be half the person I am today without you.

Lastly, but oh, so importantly; Sophia: What we have cannot be reduced to the written word or a token of thanks. I do not know where I end and you begin.

Jacket photo outtake. Apparently, posing makes me sneeze . . . (photograph by Sophie Hart)

Last day, taking it all in with Troian Bellisario. We began the journey together as two kids fresh out of drama school. Now we're old. Just. Old.

This photo was taken by yours truly on Keegan's last day. Oddly, I didn't cry in any of the farewell moments with the rest of the cast. The only time I shed a tear was right after this photo was taken. Keegan looked me in the face, sighed, and said, "Well, I guess we're done man. . . ."